Creative Parenting

393
Positive Parenting Ideas
to Help your Child Grow

Jed Jurchenko

www.CoffeeShopConversations.com

Dedication

To parenting committed to learning,
growing, parenting with creativity, and
raising great kids.

Also by Jed

131 Creative Conversations for Couples

131 Engaging Conversations for Couples

131 Creative Conversations for Families

131 Conversations for Stepfamily Success

131 Connecting Conversations
for Parents and Teens

Happy Skills for Happy Kids

Becoming Brave:
How Little Buffalo Finds His Courage

The Stormy Secret

Addison Goes to Butterfly School

Get Free Books

To thank you for your purchase, I would like to send you a bonus gift.

Transform from discouraged and burned out to an enthusiastic agent of joy who parents at a higher, happier level. *Be Happier Now* provides ten easy to apply happiness strategies for reducing stress and increasing joy at home!

I will also make sure you are the first to know about free books and future deals!

www.CoffeeShopConversations.com/happiness

Contents

131

Conversations That Engage Kids

How to Get Kids Talking, Grow Their Friendships, and Inspire Change

Jed Jurchenko

www.CoffeeShopConversations.com

Dedication

Dedicated to parents, stepparents, foster parents, teachers, mentors, and coaches who tirelessly build into the lives of kids.

Dedicated to the children and tweens striving to build face-to-face connections in an increasingly virtual world.

Dedicated to my own children, Mackenzie, Brooklyn, Addison, and Emmalynn. May your contagious joy, compassion for others, and desire to be good friends continue to grow!

131
Conversations That Engage Kids

***

The Big Deal
about Small Talk

Welcome to *131 Conversations That Engage Kids*, a small book with the big goal of getting kids talking and keeping them engaged. This book is for two primary audiences. First, it is for adults who want to help children build strong connections in an increasingly virtual and disconnected world. This includes parents, stepparents, foster parents, teachers, coaches, youth pastors, and mentors. Second, this book is for children and tweens longing to build face-to-face friendships that develop into lifelong bonds.

There are four important reasons for getting intentional about face-to-face conversation. First, conversations create a connection. Second, they influence positive life change. Third, conversations build social skills, and fourth, they are a whole lot of fun. The conversation starters in this book are practically guaranteed to get your kids talking and keep them engaged. However, before diving in, let's first examine why each of these areas is so important!

Goal #1: Talking to Connect

Conversation is one of the primary ways that people connect. This is true for both children and adults. Psychology uses the term *attachment* to describe the close bonding that takes place among family members and friends. Multiple studies have concluded that a secure attachment results in lower levels of anxiety, depression, and worry. It also leads to increased levels of success in college and better interpersonal relationships throughout one's lifetime.[1] In this book, the words *attachment* and *connection* are used interchangeably. Connection is important because, as students of human behavior know, connection changes everything!

The Connection Advantage

Connection is what allows a petite, five-foot mother to keep her six-foot-tall athletic son in check. When the teenage years arrive, physically enforcing rules at home becomes increasingly difficult. One does not simply pick up a teenager and set them in time-out and attempting to do so would be foolish. Placing incessant restrictions on beloved items such as cell phones, extracurricular activities, and household privileges is exhausting. Fortunately, a strong bond between parent and child can render these methods unnecessary. I am acquainted with a number of teens who follow the rules not because they have to nor because they want to but because they cannot stand the thought of breaking their mom or dad's heart.

A strong attachment is what causes friends and family to stick together through thick and thin. It is also the reason why sports teams give 110 percent. When children are connected, they push themselves over, above, and beyond what they feel capable of accomplishing, because when someone we are connected to believes that we are capable, we believe it too. In short, attachment is the foundation of multiple types of success.

Attachment Metaphors

There are two excellent metaphors for attachment. First, attachment is an invisible string that crosses cities, states, oceans, and continents. This unseen bond allows children to feel loved, even when they are a great distance away.

Second, a strong attachment is like a revitalizing well of water in the midst of a scorching wasteland. Kind words submerge themselves deep into our children's hearts and are later drawn upon for strength and comfort. Object relation therapists use the word *introjection* to describe the internal connection to others that continues throughout life.

Connection and Intimacy

Although nearly everyone longs for close connections, not everyone knows how to cultivate them. A sunflower requires water, oxygen, sunlight, rich soil, and time to blossom. Similarly, positive attachments require time, consistency, and mutual intimacy.

Although intimacy is an odd term for a book for preteens, our definition fits nicely. In this book, intimacy is defined as "in-to-me-see." It is the act of allowing another person to peer into one's inner world while simultaneously sharing one's own heart. Intimacy covers the entire gamut of a person's inner life by starting shallow and deepening over time. Attachment begins with face-to-face conversation and is the glue that binds people together through all the ups and downs of life.

For preteens, having safe adults and positive peers to share their inner world with is especially important. As we will see in this next goal, the people our children are closest to have a big part in steering which direction they will go.

Goal #2: Talking for Change

Conversation is a key that unlocks positive life change and dynamic personal growth. Although the conversations in this book do not push for change directly, they do create an environment where growth is possible. Let me explain with a simple illustration. A car cruising down the highway in the wrong direction can easily get back on track with a few turns of the steering wheel. On the other hand, a car stuck in the mud or at a broken standstill requires a great deal effort to reach its destination—even if that car is pointed in the right direction.

Similarly, preteens who are actively engaged in conversations with positive adults can be gently guided in the right direction. On the other hand, supporting youth who are checked-out is a daunting task. I know this from years of personal experience. Crossed arms, avoidance of eye contact, and a glazed-over look are barriers to growth that no amount of logic, lectures, or life wisdom will penetrate. Re-engagement is required first. Then, and only then, can growth occur. This book is about "fueling the car," so you can steer the conversation where it needs to go.

If you already have engaged kids and want to take the next steps, be sure to check out my book *131 Creative Conversations for Families*. This resource hones in on value-based conversations that promote wisdom and maturity in thirteen different areas of life. However, because these conversations focus on growth and not engagement, it is a good idea to start with the conversations in this book and to deepen your dialogue over time.

Goal #3: Building Social Skills

Basic social skills are no longer as basic as they once were, and many are becoming a lost art. Virtual relationships via text, email, and social media are the new norm. Parents who spent their childhood playing dress-up with friends, creating imaginary worlds, and having outdoor adventures until the streetlights came on bemoan how their preteens gather together, only to zone out in front of their electronic devices.

Today's kids are simultaneously more connected and more disconnected than any prior generation. Long-distance friendships come easily, while face-to-face connections can be scary. The conversation starters in this book provide the opportunity to practice the communication skills that do not come as naturally to the electronically savvy. Here are five key conversational micro-skills to reinforce while going through this book:

1. Gentle Eye Contact:

It is said that the eyes are the window to the soul. Eye contact nonverbally communicates "You are important." One's gaze should be confident, warm, and natural. Finding that balance between laser-like intensity and distracted wandering comes with practice.

2. Keep an Open Posture:

It is estimated that as much as 93 percent of communication is nonverbal.[2] Communicate warmth and interest by keeping an open posture. Turn your body toward the other person, with arms and legs uncrossed. This simple gesture says, "I am open to hearing what you have to say."

3. Listen Actively:

Active listening involves drawing out the speaker's story with simple affirmations. This includes head nods, a soft smile, and verbal "uh-huhs" that inform the speaker you are tracking with what is said.

4. Appreciate Differences:

Face-to-face conversations are the perfect time to practice appreciating differences. If you and your friend were alike in every way, then one of you would not be necessary. It is entirely possible to listen empathetically and considerately even if you do not agree with every point made. Knowing how to listen to a variety of opinions in a respectful manner is an exceptionally valuable skill to master.

5. Draw the Speaker Out:

Finally, draw the speaker out with good follow-up questions. Do not just act interested, be interested. The easiest way to accomplish this is to get curious about the other person's perspective. Everyone has unique life experiences from which we can learn. Our job is to draw their story out.

Goal #4: Talking for Fun

Finally, talking is fun, and having fun is a big deal. In fact, it is so important that the renowned therapist William Glasser, the founder of choice theory, considered it one of the five basic human needs. Having fun is essential for at least three reasons.

First, children mature through play and fun. Second, fun is a stress reliever that greatly benefits our mental health. The diathesis-stress model of mental illness suggests that high levels of stress increase the chance of mental illness. This means that having fun may keep you from driving yourself crazy — literally! Finally, as you probably already know, fun is a powerful relationship builder. Fun times create fantastic memories, which lead to lasting friendships.

Appropriate humor and a playful attitude are powerful allies in nearly every area of life. If you are not having fun, then you are doing things wrong. Although the conversations in this book are designed to be fun, funny, interesting, and highly engaging, here are some additional strategies for getting the most out of the pages ahead:

1. Conversation Jenga

Purchase a Jenga game (or a similar type of block-stacking game) if you do not own one already. Using a marker, write a number on each block (or write the numbers on small stickers and attach them to each block). Next, build the tower and follow the usual instructions, with one simple twist. After each person removes a block from the tower, that person must answer the question that corresponds to the number on his or her block.

2. Conversation Beach Ball

Inflate a beach ball, and using a permanent marker, write the numbers 1–131 on the ball. The position of the numbers on the ball is unimportant, so long as the numbers cover a large portion of the ball's surface. To start the game, toss the beach ball to a family member or friend. The person who catches the ball must locate the number closest to their right thumb and answer the corresponding question in this book. Then they should toss the ball to the next player.

3. Conversation Balloon Pop

This icebreaker is perfect for parties and high-energy engagement. Either make copies of your favorite questions or write the number of those questions on a thin strip of paper. Next, place one strip of paper inside of each balloon and inflate it. Have fun bouncing the balloons back and forth, mixing up the conversation starters. Take turns popping the balloons and answering the questions inside.

Other strategies for getting the most out of this book include going through the questions over dinner or before bedtime (which is often one of the easiest times to get a conversation going). You could also store this book in the car for use on road trips or use it consistently during the daily drive to school.

The most important thing is to take pleasure in the process. This book is not a task to complete but a journey to be enjoyed. There is no prize for finishing every question, no timeline, no penalty for skipping over conversation starters that don't resonate with you, and nothing miraculous happens when the book is complete. The real magic is in the process itself. So take your time and have fun, every step of the way!

Sincerely,

COFFEE SHOP CONVERSATIONS

131
Conversations That Engage Kids

*While we try to teach our children
all about life, our children teach us
what life is all about.*

~ Angela Schwindt, homeschooling mom

*Children are great imitators.
So give them something great to imitate.*

~ Anonymous

Conversation #1

If you were president of the United States for a day, what law you would enact or change?

Conversation #2

If you took a sneak peek at Santa's list, do you think you would find your name on the naughty or nice list, and why?

Conversation #3

If you had the opportunity to ask God a single question, what would it be?

Conversation #4

Which of *The Seven Dwarfs* best describes you today—Bashful, Dopey, Sleepy, Sneezy, Grumpy, Happy, or Doc?

Conversation #5

If you could travel back in time and spend the day with one historical figure, who would it be, and why?

Conversation #6

What is one book you believe every child should read?

Conversation #7

If you had to choose one food to eat every single day for the next year, what would it be?

Conversation #8

In the book *Wonder*, Mr. Browne's precept for the month of October states, "Your deeds are your monuments." What is one of your monuments that makes you especially proud?

Conversation #9

If you took the place of the girl Riley Anderson in the cartoon *Inside Out*, which emotion would be at your controls most often—Joy, Sadness, Fear, Disgust, or Anger?

Conversation #10

If you had to choose between going through the rest of your life not being able to see or not being able to hear, which would you choose, and why?

Conversation #11

If you could have any superpower, what would it be, and how would you use this skill for good?

Conversation #12

What is one simple pleasure that made you happy today?

Conversation #13

If the zoo offered to let you keep an exotic animal as a pet, what animal would you bring home with you?

Conversation #14

What is the kindest thing that someone has done for you this week?

Conversation #15

How have you been kind to someone else this week?

Conversation #16

An old precept says, "It is better to give than to receive." Do you believe this statement is true? Why, or why not?

Conversation #17

How do people know when they are in love? When you fall in love, how will you know?

Conversation #18

Some people make a "bucket list," or a list of things they hope to do and see before they die. What are two things you would put on your bucket list?

Conversation #19

In the book *The Adventures of Tom Sawyer,* Tom and his friend Huck Finn sneak into their own funeral and listen to their eulogies. Imagine that, like Tom and Huck, you have the opportunity to listen in at your own funeral. What do you hope your friends and family say about you?

Conversation #20

If you had the opportunity to give one piece of advice to our current president, what would it be?

Conversation #21

What do you think happens to people immediately after they die?

Conversation #22

If you inherited Superman's ability to fly for a single day—and only for one day—where would you go, and what would you do?

Conversation #23

In the movie *Frozen*, Elsa has power over ice and snow. Instead of embracing this gift, she conceals it because she is different. What makes you feel different from others and causes you to want to hide?

Conversation #24

What song makes you want to dance the most?

Conversation #25

When was the last time you said the words "I'm sorry," and what did you apologize for?

Conversation #26

What family member do you look up to, and what specifically do you admire about this person?

Conversation #27

Finish this sentence: "The best part about being me is..."

Conversation #28

Complete this sentence: "Something difficult about being me is..."

Conversation #29

Imagine that you have the ability to grant your parents one superpower. What ability would you bestow upon them, and why?

Conversation #30

What is one thing you admire about your mom or dad?

Conversation #31

What is one thing that your mom or dad say they appreciate about you?

Conversation #32

If you were asked to choose the next president of the United States, who would you appoint to run the country, and why?

Conversation #33

What cartoon character has a personality most like your own?

Conversation #34

Complete this sentence: "One food I would be happy never eating again is..."

Conversation #35

If you had to go through the rest of your life with either no arms or no legs, which one would you choose? Why?

Conversation #36

Imagine that a genie offers to grant you a single wish, and wishing for more wishes is forbidden. What would your wish be?

The only man who never makes a mistake is the man who never does anything.

~Theodore Roosevelt

Conversation #37

In the movie *Freaky Friday*, a mom and daughter switch bodies. If you woke up in your parent's body, how would you spend the day?

Conversation #38

If Santa Claus offered to give you an early Christmas present — one that you would receive this very moment — what would you ask him for?

Conversation #39

Finish this sentence, "One lesson I learned, or am learning, this year is..."

Conversation #40

Imagine that a rich relative passes away and leaves you in charge of managing his estate. Your first task is to donate a million dollars to any worthy cause you choose. How will you use this money to help others?

Conversation #41

Imagine a rich relative gives you a million dollars to spend any way you like. What is the first purchase you would make for you?

Conversation #42

If you could change one rule in your home, what would it be, and why?

Conversation #43

What is a rule in your home that you appreciate, and why do you like this rule?

Conversation #44

Imagine a famous movie producer wants to make a major motion picture about your life. You get to select a Hollywood star to play you. Whom would you choose, and why?

Conversation #45

What is something that brought you joy this week?

Conversation #46

The word *phobia* is used to describe irrational fears. Some people are terrified of spiders (arachnophobia), others are afraid of heights (acrophobia), and some panic when confined to a small space, like an elevator (claustrophobia). What irrational fear might you possess?

Conversation #47

Who is one of your best friends, and what is one thing you admire about this person?

Conversation #48

What is one thing that happened this week that was frustrating or annoying? (Even small frustrations count.)

Conversation #49

Describe a favorite holiday memory. Where did you go, what did you do, and why was this time so meaningful for you?

Conversation #50

Complete this sentence: "The most adventurous thing I did this year was..."

Conversation #51

Finish this sentence: "An injustice in our world that makes me mad is..."

Conversation #52

If you could pick a famous person to mentor you—such as a well-known athlete, musician, artist, or writer—who would you choose, and what would they teach you?

Conversation #53

Finish this sentence: "The most stressful part of being me is..."

Conversation #54

When you are feeling sad, mad, or frustrated, what activity makes you smile again?

Conversation #55

Complete this sentence, "The best part about being me is..."

Conversation #56

If you were principal of your school for a day, what is one school rule you would change?

Conversation #57

An old adage says, "Children should be seen but not heard." Do you agree or disagree with this statement, and why?

Conversation #58

Who is the bravest person you know? What do you think it is that makes this person so brave?

Conversation #59

Name one movie you think everyone ought to see. Then explain why people need to watch this movie.

Conversation #60

Walt Disney said, "If you can dream it, you can do it." If you knew, without a doubt, that you could do anything and would not fail, what would you do?

Conversation #61

In the movie *Rocky*, Rocky Balboa has a theme song that makes him feel powerful when he trains for upcoming boxing matches. What song gets you motivated and energized?

Children see magic because they look for it.

~Christopher Moore, writer

Conversation #62

An extrovert feels energized when they are around people. An introvert is refreshed by spending time alone. Do you think you are more of an extrovert or an introvert?

Conversation #63

If you had to choose one sport—and only one sport—to watch for the rest of your life, what would it be?

Conversation #64

Imagine that your parents tell you it is time to look for a part-time job. Where would enjoy working, and why?

Conversation #65

Finish this sentence: "A job I hope to never work, under any circumstances, is..."

Conversation #66

Name three qualities you possess that make you a good friend.

Conversation #67

Imagine that you wake up this Monday and discover school is canceled. How would you want to spend your day?

Conversation #68

What is your favorite subject in school, and why?

Conversation #69

What is your least favorite subject in school, and why?

Conversation #70

Imagine a rich relative offers to buy you your first car—absolutely any car you choose. What vehicle would you ask for?

Conversation #71

In the Harry Potter series, certain wizards, known as Animagi, have the ability to transform into animals. If you were an Animagus, what animal would you change into, and how would you use your power?

Conversation #72

A pet peeve is a little irritation—like biting one's fingernails or burping after a meal—that you find especially annoying. What is one of your biggest pet peeves?

Conversation #73

Sometimes adults like to say, "A penny saved is a penny earned." Do you believe this statement is true and that saving money is the same as earning money? Why?

Conversation #74

Imagine your birthday is declared a national holiday, like Thanksgiving, Christmas, or Presidents' Day. Describe how you would like people to celebrate your holiday.

Conversation #75

Steve Jobs, the former CEO of Apple Inc., recalls being asked by his fourth-grade teacher, "What is it that you don't understand about the universe?"[3] How would you answer this question?

Conversation #76

Your house is on fire! Fortunately, your family and pets are safe. Unfortunately, you only have time to grab three personal belongings before scrambling outside. What will you take with you?

Conversation #77

You can choose any musical group to play at your birthday party this year. What band do you pick, and what opening song will they play?

Conversation #78

Imagine that you are given the task of abolishing one holiday—meaning no one will be allowed to celebrate this holiday ever again, in any way, shape, or form. Which holiday will you eliminate?

Conversation #79

What is your favorite holiday, and how do you celebrate it?

Conversation #80

What is your favorite comfort food to enjoy after a stressful day? When was the last time you ate it?

Conversation #81

Surprise, you get to choose your own allergies! What two foods will you be allergic to for the rest of your life?

Conversation #82

Today everyone will call you by your favorite nickname. How will everyone refer to you?

Conversation #83

Complete this sentence: "One app, video game, or computer program I cannot do without is..."

Conversation #84

When you get in trouble, would you rather be put on phone restriction, television restriction, or internet restriction, and why?

Conversation #85

Finish this sentence: "An unusual talent I have is..."

Conversation #86

Tell a story about a time you were embarrassed. Who was involved, and what happened?

Conversation #87

If you could travel back in time and give one piece of advice to your younger self, what advice would you give?

Conversation #88

Finish this sentence. "Parents should always..."

Conversation #89

Finish this sentence. "Parents should never..."

Conversation #90

If you could spend the day binge-watching any television series, what show would you watch?

Conversation #91

What movie do you hope they make a sequel to, soon?

Conversation #92

What movie is so bad that it should never, under any circumstances, have a sequel made?

Conversation #93

Tomorrow, you have the option of going skydiving, scuba diving, or staying home and watching television. What activity would you choose, and why?

Conversation #94

Surprise, you get to compete on any game show you want! Which one will you choose, and why?

Conversation #95

What bad habit are you currently trying to break?

Conversation #96

What is one healthy habit that you have?

Conversation #97

You will soon be stranded on a tropical island for a year and get to take one luxury item with you. What will you bring, and why?

Conversation #98

You are about to be stranded on a deserted island for a year and get to bring one music album with you. What album will you take?

Conversation #99

You are about to be stranded on a deserted island for a year and get to bring one — and only one — book with you. Which book will you choose?

Conversation #100

The Elf on the Shelf came early this year and has been watching you all week. Now he is reporting back to Santa. Describe a high point of the week that Santa will hear about.

"Children are great imitators. So give them something great to imitate."

~Anonymous

Conversation #101

The Elf on the Shelf came early this year and has been watching you all week. Now he is reporting back to Santa. Describe a low point of the week that Santa will hear about.

Conversation #102

No two snowflakes are exactly alike. No two people are the same either. What is something that makes you unique or special?

Conversation #103

Do you usually remember your dreams or forget them? If you remember them, describe one dream you are able to recall.

Conversation #104

Describe a favorite family holiday tradition.

Conversation #105

Describe an all-time favorite Halloween costume. What did you dress up as, why did you like this costume, and how did others react to it?

Conversation #106

Describe a happy memory from a favorite family vacation.

Conversation #107

Finish this sentence: "The world would be a better place if..."

Conversation #108

Complete this phrase: "Something many people don't know about me is..."

Conversation #109

If your life was turned into a book, what would the title of your story be?

Conversation #110

If your life was turned into a book, where in the bookstore would it be found (drama, comedy, adventure, romance, suspense, etc.), and why?

Conversation #111

What was the worst injury you ever had, and how did it happen?

Conversation #112

Imagine that you peer into a crystal ball that allows you to peek ten years into the future. Describe what you see.

Conversation #113

In your opinion, what is the perfect combination of pizza toppings?

Conversation #114

In your opinion, at what age should children have privilege and responsibility of a smartphone, and why?

Conversation #115

In your opinion, what flavor of ice cream should never be invented?

Conversation #116

If you could visit any country in the world, which country would it be? Why?

Conversation #117

Which pieces of Halloween candy do you always eat first?

Conversation #118

What is one thing you did in the last month to make this world a better place? (Even little acts are OK.)

Conversation #119

What dish or meal would you like to learn how to cook?

Conversation #120

Imagine you are a guest contestant on the latest reality cooking show, where you are asked to whip up your specialty. Thinking about everything you know how to make, what dish do you consider your specialty?

Conversation #121

What flavor of ice cream would you gladly eat every day for an entire year?

Conversation #122

Do you use any form of social media, such as Facebook, Twitter, or Instagram? If so, which one is your favorite, and why?

Conversation #123

Anthony Brandt said, "Other things may change us, but we start and end with family." Describe something you love about your family.

Conversation #124

What is your least favorite or most dreaded form of exercise?

Conversation #125

If you made a New Year's resolution today, what would your resolution be?

Conversation #126

In your opinion, what does the perfect New Year's celebration look like?

Conversation #127

Imagine you are sent to work for the circus for one year. The good news is that you can choose your act and the circus performers will train you. What act will you be performing for the next year, and why?

Conversation #128

What future activity, vacation, or event are you most excited about right now?

Conversation #129

What video game does every adult need to play at least once in their lifetime?

Conversation #130

What is one helpful piece of advice your parents, teacher, or a friend gave you?

Conversation #131

Animals are used to represent the four different personality types. This includes 1) The Lion: A confident leader, who takes charge of tasks and makes sure things get done; 2) the Otter: Outgoing, playful, and creative, the otter is the life of the party; 3) the Beaver: Detail-oriented and organized, the beaver is excellent at helping others stay on task; 4) the Golden Retriever: Warm and friendly, the golden retriever genuinely cares for others. Which personality type best describes you?

Connecting in a
Disconnected World

When it comes to communicating and connecting, kids cannot afford to be average. Not only is average boring, but average also does not work. If you have any doubt, consider the following statistics. According to a poll of two thousand families, the average family spends less than eight hours together each week.[4] This boils down to a mere thirty-six minutes on weekdays and about five hours together over the weekend. The fact that much of this time is spent zoned out in front of the television or internet or honed-in on cell phones only amplifies the problem.

Studies show that tweens, or children between the ages of eight and twelve, spend an average of six hours a day in front of a screen. In fact, some thirteen-year-olds report checking their social media accounts as much as one hundred times a day.[5] With these statistics in mind, it is not surprising that face-to-face communication skills have declined.

If you purchased this book for your own home, then you have already set your family apart from the norm. If you are using this book to encourage the kids that you mentor, coach, or teach to connect better, then you are likely already well aware of the challenges mentioned and know how important developing relationships is.

Now that you have reached the end of this book, the next step is to keep the conversations going. Fortunately, this can be easy. Children are continually developing and changing, so it is perfectly acceptable to return to the same conversations often. As life experiences are gained, feelings and opinions alter. Soon, fresh insights will spice up old conversations.

In short, there is simply too much connecting to do for kids and families to check out. This is something you almost certainly already know. However, sometimes it is helpful to have our ideas reaffirmed by someone else. The bottom line is that now that this book is complete, keep asking good questions and keep encouraging the kids around you to connect. Wishing you a multitude of happy conversations in the days ahead!

Sincerely,

COFFEE SHOP CONVERSATIONS

End Notes

1. Vivona, Jeanine M. "Parental Attachment Styles of Late Adolescents: Qualities of Attachment Relationships and Consequences for Adjustment," *Journal of Counseling Psychology* 2000, Vol. 47, No. 3, 327.

2. Mehrabian, Albert. *Silent Messages: Implicit Communications of Emotions and Attitudes,* Wadsworth Publishing Company, July 1972. Albert suggests that words account for 7% of communication, tone of voice 38%, and body language 55%.

3. Isaacson, Walter. *Steve Jobs,* Simon & Schuster, October 2011.

4. McCann, Jaymi. "No time for the family? You are not alone: Parents and children spend less than an hour with each other every day because of modern demands." *The Daily Mail,* July 2013, http://www.dailymail.co.uk/news/article-2363193/No-time-family-You-Parents-

children-spend-hour-day-modern-demands.html#ixzz4ZAR107Ui.

5. Wallace, Kelly. "Teens spend a 'mind-boggling' 9 hours a day using media, report says." CNN, November 3, 2013. http://www.cnn.com/2015/11/03/health/teens-tweens-media-screen-use-report.

131
Boredom Busters and Creativity Builders for Kids

Inspire your kids to exercise their imagination, expand their creativity, and have an awesome childhood!

Jed Jurchenko

www.CoffeeShopConversations.com

Dedication

Dedicated to parents, stepparents, foster parents, teachers, mentors, and coaches who tirelessly build into the lives of kids.

Dedicated to the children and tweens who are actively engaging with others, growing their responsibility, and staying creative in an increasingly busy and virtual world.

Dedicated to my own children, Mackenzie, Brooklyn, Addison, and Emmalynn.
May your adventuresome spirits, creativity, and love for life continue to grow!

.

131 Boredom Busters and Creativity Builders for Kids

Chapter 1:

Chapter 2:

Chapter 3:

Chapter 4:

Chapter 5:

The Power of Play

Although it is only 10:30 a.m., I am exhausted. My wife, Jenny, and I have been awake for most of the night. We are in the hospital's emergency room with Addison, our three-year-old daughter. She has a painful rash that is causing her skin to char and peel.

The bright side is that, after an excruciating night, the medications are finally bringing some relief. Much to my delight, little Addison is in better spirits overall. About an hour ago, a nurse gave her a stuffed baby owlet, which she promptly named after herself. When breakfast arrived, I spoon-fed Addison scrambled eggs and Cheerios. Even with the pain medications, any movement causes her body to throb, preventing Addison from feeding herself.

Soon, Addison, who has a superb imagination, decides that she is an owlet too and begins hooting between bites. It lifts everyone's spirits to see her having fun. This moment of play, in the midst of endless doctors, nurses, and IVs, is refreshing.

Now that breakfast is over, I plant myself in a chair beside Addison's bed, where she has fallen asleep. Sleep is a good sign. According to the doctors, it is when her body will heal itself the fastest.

In the bed to my left, Jenny has also dozed off. This is another positive since she, too, needs to recuperate from the overwhelming stress of this recent turn of events. For me, this moment of stillness is the perfect opportunity to write. Although a hospital stay is an unusual time to begin a book, writing is one way that I manage stress. Putting words on paper is a healing experience. This means that you and I are on this journey together, because helping families heal is one of the many reasons I am writing this book.

Healing Play

As a marriage and family therapist and a former children's pastor, I have witnessed the healing power of play on countless occasions. Just as medical doctors know that sleep is necessary to recover from physical maladies, therapists understand that play promotes healing from past traumas, as well as from the everyday stressors of life. It is how children work through their worries, frustrations, anger, and fear.

Likely, Addison's imitation of an owlet is her way of communicating the helplessness she feels. Adults connect with family and friends in order to talk about their problems. Even when issues are not fully resolved, the simple act of being understood by someone we are bonded with is revitalizing.

Play with Purpose

While adults talk out their troubles, children play out theirs, often returning to the same themes until they find a resolution. This means that play is much more than fun and games. It is a primary way that children heal emotionally, and very serious business.

Unfortunately, as you may have already observed with your own children–or other kids that you know–creative play is gradually becoming a lost art. On the one hand, playing is a natural part of childhood. On the other hand, in our fast-paced, technologically advanced, and highly structured society, creative play is vanishing amid a myriad of activities and digital entertainment options that are more readily available than ever before.

In upcoming chapters, I share insights gleaned from our family's journey from overly scheduled and hyper-entertained to rediscovering the simple joys of life. Then we will dive into 131 boredom busters and creativity builders. These ideas are designed to promote a spirit of active engagement, increased responsibility, and family unity.

Three Types of Activities

Some of the activities in this book will strongly resonate with your family, while others may be less popular. This is precisely why so many options are included. There is no need to implement every idea. Simply select the ones that fit your family's style and culture the best.

This book is about playing with a purpose. Each boredom buster and creativity builder is founded on a key principle. Many of the activities are highly engaging, some promote an increased sense of responsibility, while others do an especially good job of exercising the imagination. A few of the activities fit into all three categories at once. Now let's examine why each of these areas is so important.

Activities that Engage

It was a chilly winter evening, and bedtime was quickly approaching. However, on this particular night, Jenny had something different in mind. After calling our family into the kitchen, where steaming mugs of hot chocolate awaited, she produced a tray filled with hundreds of marshmallows–both large and small–and boxes of brightly colored toothpicks. Jenny enthusiastically announced, "We are going to have a marshmallow-sculpturing contest!"

It is amazing what a family can create out of marshmallows, toothpicks, and a little imagination. It is also astounding how fun this simple project can be. That evening, our kitchen table overflowed with joy as we talked, created, and stuffed our mouths with far too much sugar.

Some of the ideas in this book are included simply because they are fun. These activities are designed to motivate your children to pause their electronics, fully engage in the moment, and build an abundance of happy memories!

Activities That Promote Responsibility

Over the past twenty years, I have worked with families in a variety of roles, including marriage and family therapist, children's pastor, and camp counselor. As a way of continuing my own growth, I participate in a number of conferences each year. During my early days of family work, I attended a memorable workshop where the speaker homed in on the value of having a family laundry day. The way he described the event made doing laundry together sound like the latest ride at Disneyland. To be honest, it was a little weird.

Fast-forward five years. Life is busier than ever. Although Jenny and I are moving at a rapid pace, we are continuing to fall behind. It feels like we are trapped in a scene from the Star Wars movie, the one where Han Solo and Princess Leah escape down the garbage chute, only to have the walls of the trash compactor slowly close in on them. Laundry and other household chores are piling up, slowly squeezing our family out of our own home.

For some reason, the family laundry story comes to mind. I recall the presenter's preaching on the importance of togetherness, the value of passing on an essential life skill from one generation to the next, and the moments of joy that transpire along the way. Although I have my doubts, we are desperate, and there is one thing that I know with certainty: the laundry is not going to fold itself. So out of desperation, I take the speaker's admonition to heart.

After calling our children into the family room, I dump a pile of freshly washed clothing onto the couch, announcing, "It's family laundry day," with as much enthusiasm as I can muster. Seeing the mountain of clothes, the girls' faces drop.

Initially, there are groans and some dragging of the feet, but ultimately, the sorting and hanging begins. I bring in more laundry, and soon we are folding together. At some point, the stereo is turned on. Heads start bobbing, and the girls sing along. By the time the last garment is placed in its drawer, a full-blown dance party has erupted. Surprisingly, doing the laundry together worked. The clothes are put away, and there are moments of joy in the process. Mission accomplished!

In the spirit of honesty, you should know that our family does not always fold laundry together, and when we do, you will never hear anyone suggest that this is the highlight of their week. Nevertheless, I include this simple illustration because folding laundry is one example of a boredom buster that builds responsibility.

One of our duties as parents is to guide our children toward becoming responsible adults. Simple household chores are one way of accomplishing this. Family responsibilities also help children to internalize the importance of their role within the family unit. In my work with foster families, I suggest assigning daily tasks to everyone in the home because these duties communicate, "Our family is a team where everyone has a crucial role to play."

Permission to Parent Responsibly

Years ago, when that workshop presenter shared his family laundry experiences, I felt like I was granted permission to follow his lead. While parents do not need permission to guide their children to become responsible adults, it helped me to understand that I am not alone on this journey.

As you probably know, parenting comes with an ample amount of guilt attached. Some parents try to offset their overly strict childhoods by being excessively permissive with their children. Foster parents may feel bad about the past pain their foster children endured and overly compensate by doing too much for them.

Stepparents, particularly stepmothers, are also especially vulnerable. Caring stepmoms may shy away from asking their children to help, out of fear of receiving the dreaded label of "evil stepmother" that is propagated in so many fairy tales—think *Cinderella*, *Snow White*, and *Hansel and Gretel*.

In this book, I would like to pass on the same gift that the speaker gave to me. I want to grant you permission to have your children pause their electronics and take on responsibilities at home. Not only will this help your kids grow, but they will also be happier as a result.

In the pages ahead, we will dive into strategies for encouraging increased responsibility in a creative, playful, and none-too-painful manner. As you assign responsibility-building tasks to your children, you may be pleasantly surprised at just how much they are able to accomplish!

Activities That Expand the Imagination

Finally, this book contains activities that expand the imagination. You will find that most of the craft-related activities suggest using items that you already have at home. This is done intentionally, to foster ingenuity.

Do you remember playing with Legos as a kid? If your childhood was similar to mine, then chances are you can recall a time when you wanted a specific piece but could not find it among the masses of other Legos. After sifting through the pieces, you would discover a block that was not an exact fit, but it was close enough, so you made it work. Because the part did not fit perfectly, cunning resourcefulness would kick in. This would lead to new ideas and result in the creation turning out even better than imagined.

The same principle applies to this book. When our children do not have all the materials they desire and are encouraged to figure it out, their creative minds spring into action. The problem-solving capabilities of the human brain are astounding and something that we parents would be wise to encourage.

Employees who think outside the box, and who get the job done under less-than-ideal circumstances, are in high demand. Parents can cultivate these critical-thinking skills early on by expressing confidence that their child can find a solution.

As you can see, engaging, imaginative, and responsibility-building play has plenty of benefits. Play is healing. It advances social skills, grows relationships, and helps our children to succeed in life. The best part is that this is accomplished while our children have loads of fun along the way.

Nevertheless, the transition from overly scheduled and hyper-entertained to a balanced approach—where unstructured free time and imagination are honored—is not always easy. In the next chapter, I share how our family's journey began.

Ingredients of an Awesome Childhood

A soft smile stretches across Jenny's face as she recounts the joys of growing up in a small town in Minnesota. Her parents would order her and her sisters to "Go play outside, and don't come back in until we call for you." Jenny recalls spending hours reading in her favorite tree, swimming in the river that meandered through the far side of her yard and inventing new dance moves with her friends. Jenny's parents believed that it was safe and healthy for kids to spend plenty of time outdoors, and Jenny has loads of awesome childhood memories because of this.

I, on the other hand, grew up in far different surroundings. My grandfather had moved to the city of Lemon Grove when my dad was a child. During this time, there were an abundance of lemon trees, dairy farms, and wide-open spaces. However, by the time

I was born, the town had expanded to the point that it seamlessly connected to the neighboring communities of San Diego County. Housing developments had consumed the lemon orchards, and a massive concrete lemon was erected as a tribute to what used to be. With a continually expanding population of over three million people, San Diego County feels like one massive city.

Unlike Jenny, my childhood did not include streams, fields, and wide-open spaces. Fortunately, my siblings and I did have a large backyard to explore. Then, as I grew older, the biking adventures began. On weekends, my friend Loren and I would ride for hours. Mt. Helix, a local landmark with an elevation gain of over one thousand feet, was a favorite biking challenge. After doing the strenuous climb, then pausing to catch our breath and enjoy the awe-inspiring view, the two of us would race down at full speed, often overtaking cars in the process.

On other days, the two of us would pedal to the local arcade or to a nearby fabricated lake. Like Jenny, I, too, had many incredible childhood adventures.

An Awesome Foundation

Jenny and I both have fond memories of outdoor freedom, make-believe, and discovery. These ingredients are the highlights of childhood. But don't take my word for it. All of the classic children's stories agree. In the books *Tom Sawyer*, *Anne of Green Gables*, *Alice in Wonderland*, *The Chronicles of Narnia*, and the modern-day *Harry Potter*, the adventures always begin when life is unplanned.

Could you imagine what would have happened if Susan, Peter, Edmund, and Lucy had owned high-tech tablets? There would have been no game of hide-and-seek, no reason to explore the magical wardrobe, and Narnia would have remained undiscovered. In fact, had C.S. Lewis grown up in the twenty-first century, Narnia may have never existed.

In college, I read *Surprised by Joy*, a book where C.S. Lewis reminisces about his youth. He describes the formation of his make-believe animal world, a favorite pastime that laid the foundation for his acclaimed Narnia series.

- Freedom
- Creativity
- Daydreaming
- Messiness
- Adventure
- Friendship
- Boredom
- Problem-solving
- Laughter
  Imagination

These magical ingredients make childhood awesome! Youth is one of the few times when it is perfectly acceptable to color outside of the lines. The downside of a busy childhood is that many of these things are stripped away. I know this because I am a daddy of four girls and have witnessed the disease of busyness invade our own home. Sadly, the hurried life has become so routine that it regularly goes unnoticed.

Examples of increased busyness stretch far and wide. During a recent CPR training, I learned from our health-conscious instructor that while my generation received roughly ten childhood vaccinations, today's children get bombarded with over thirty. When I was in high school, I loved our church's youth group. For this reason, I was saddened to hear our youth pastor confide that he is hesitant to run events because the teenagers in his church are too busy to participate.

Parents no longer face the challenge of finding activities for their kids. The new difficulty is selecting which events they will attend. From healthcare to church, sports, schooling, and leisure activities, there is a never-ending supply of hustle and bustle available.

The bright side is that this does reduce boredom and occasionally makes life easier for us parents—I am sure that I am not the only one who entertains his screaming toddler with his smartphone. The downside is that too much glitz and glamour reduces the need for creativity. This causes me to wonder, *What if all of this stuff is robbing our children of joy?*

Reclaiming Awesome

Our family's journey to reclaiming awesome began a few years ago with a trip to Arizona. After packing up our minivan, we made the five-hour trek to the girls' great-grandparents' home. The drive was an adventure in itself, with the children routinely asking, "Are we there yet?" along the way. When we finally arrived, our girls hastily discovered they had more free time than usual.

The first two days were a difficult transition. Restlessness abounded, and the phrase "I'm bored" was blurted out often. Then, on day three, the magic happened. First, our girls began reading more. So much so that they became lost in their books. Next came socializing with adults and the trying out of new things. Our older daughters learned how to throw a Frisbee with their uncle and baked with their grandma.

Before long, their creativity kicked into high gear. There were art projects, journaling, and dressing up. Our girls even played board games together—a spectacle rarely seen at home. Jenny and I watched with delight as simple childhood joys enveloped our children.

During this trip, I discovered that sometimes the best thing I can do for my kids is to help them slow down. The lazy Arizona days passed far too quickly. We traveled back home, and just as quickly as it had left, the hustle and bustle returned.

There were sporting practices to attend, school assignments to complete, and plenty of screen time. Blaming this nonstop movement on everyone else would be dishonest. Much of the responsibility for this overly rushed pace originated with me. Fortunately, this was only the beginning of our journey. I will fill you in on the rest of the story in the following chapters.

Flexing Creativity at Home

"Daddy, I'm booored." Brooklyn drawls out her words with a mischievous smile. I know exactly what she is doing. Brooklyn is attempting to activate the boredom jar. This brightly colored container, holding nearly one hundred Popsicle sticks, sits strategically on top of our refrigerator. Scrawled on each one is a single activity that encourages our children to flex their creativity. The boredom jar is activated whenever the words "I'm bored" are spoken or whenever our children need a creativity boost.

In our home, the boredom jar is ruthless. Once activated, there is no turning back. A typical scenario plays out like this:

- One of our children utters the words "I'm bored."
- The child who made the offending statement must select a popsicle stick out of the jar.

- The creative assignment is read aloud, and the entire house is placed on lock-down until the task is complete.

Jenny and I wish that we didn't have to be so firm, but it is not our decision (at least this is the story that we tell our kids). Until the activity is complete, there is no television, no snack time, and no family games. The assigned task becomes the sole focus, and teamwork amongst siblings is highly encouraged. Brooklyn loves this game. Mackenzie is more apprehensive, yet never fails to engage.

Jenny created the boredom jar a few weeks after our trip to Arizona. To be honest, the jar sat on a shelf for a long time before it was implemented. However, once put into practice, this strategy worked better than imagined–making us wonder why we waited so long. The first time the boredom jar was activated, Jenny and I watched with delight as our two older girls teamed up to create a fantastic Lego city. They had loads of fun in the process.

Our family is learning that creativity–just like any other muscle—must be exercised regularly or it will atrophy. The more our children use their imaginations, the stronger their imaginations become.

Inspiring Creativity at Home

So why don't parents encourage their children to be creative more often? I believe that one of the biggest reasons for this is guilt. Jenny wrote about her struggle with mommy guilt on our blog, where it remains one of the most popular on the site. This is a good indication that Jenny is not alone in her struggle. I know that many dads feel guilty too. Moreover, if you live in a blended family home, as we do, then guilt is even more complicated.

For many years, my two oldest daughters lived with us for only half the week. I would feel bad about the missed time with them and had a tendency to overdo things. I would overload the first half of my week with projects so that I could be more available to them during the second half. I dreaded hearing the words, "Daddy I'm bored," and would rush in like Superman to save the day. However, I have learned that this is not always what is best.

Slowly but surely, I am learning that while children need interactive play with their parents, it is perfectly acceptable for our children to see them hard at work too. Today, I strive to model a more balanced work-hard and then play-hard approach.

Finding Work, Life, and Family Balance

Not long ago, the children and I watched the *Little House on the Prairie* series. The story revolves around the adventures of the Ingalls family raising their children in the 1870s. "Pa," played by Michael Landon, is a loving, hardworking dad, who is often in the fields from sunrise to sunset. This left him little time for hands-on involvement. In the past, many daddies parented with this traditional approach.

I, on the other hand, dove headfirst into the opposite extreme. Feeling guilty over lost time, I strove to take advantage of every second together we had. Today I know balance is best. My children need an active hands-on daddy. They also need to know that both their dad and stepmom work hard to provide for the family.

This means that it is perfectly acceptable to let the children play, and even be bored, while we parents work. This is true for two reasons. First, it is essential for parents to model the value of hard work to their children. Second, free time allows children the opportunity to exercise their imaginations.

The boredom jar is one way that I lay aside my parenting guilt and allow my kids to flex their creativity. In the next chapter, we dive into 131 engaging, creative, responsibility-building strategies. There are numerous ways that you can put these activities into action. You can build your own boredom jar, schedule a regular family activity night, or keep this book handy for whenever your children need a creativity boost.

Most of the activities can be done individually, with siblings and friends, or as a family unit. There is not one correct way to use this book. Now it is time to take action. I wish you and your family much success on your boredom-busting and creativity-building journey!

131
Boredom Busters and Creativity Builders

There is a garden in every childhood,
an enchanted place where colors are brighter,
the air softer, and the morning more fragrant
than ever again.

~ Elizabeth Lawrence

Sweet childish days,
that were as long as twenty days are now.

~ William Wordsworth, "To a Butterfly"

It is never too late to have a happy childhood.

~ Tom Robbins

Buster & Builder #1

Create your own book of "would you rather" questions. These questions require readers to choose between two difficult and often absurd options. For example, "Would you rather grow a third eye in the middle of your forehead or have a third arm grow out of your belly button?" Then test out your questions on family and friends.

Buster & Builder #2

Have an indoor campout. Set up your camping tent, use art supplies to create an indoor campfire, break out the flashlights, and cook s'mores (15 seconds in the microwave usually does the trick).

Buster & Builder #3

Create a catapult from items you have around your home. You can turn this into a contest with friends and family by seeing who can launch a paper ball the farthest.

Buster & Builder #4

Build the largest and tallest playing card castle that you can.

Buster & Builder #5

Play an indoor game of *Around the World*. Use a wastebasket as your basketball hoop and wadded-up paper for the ball. Select at least five locations at which to stand. Then make your baskets. Keep track of how many shots it takes you to "travel around the world." Then go through the course a second time, trying to beat your high score.

Buster & Builder #6

Write a list of five goals that you want to accomplish in the next year. Then take a small action toward accomplishing one of them.

Childhood is the most beautiful
of all life's seasons.
~Author Unknown

Buster & Builder #7

Practice juggling. If you already know how, then learn a new juggling trick.

Buster & Builder #8

Juggle a soccer ball by keeping a single ball in the air, using only your feet and knees, for 10 kicks. If you can already do this, try to beat your high score.

Buster & Builder #9

Make a book of conversation starters filled with fun, funny, and creative questions that spark discussion. For example, "If you could have any superpower, what would it be and why?" Bring this book to your next family meal and try out your questions.

Buster & Builder #10

Write a story using this sentence to get you started, "If I were president for a day, three things I would change are..." Then share your story over dinner.

Buster & Builder #11

Make the world's fastest and most colorful paper airplane.

Buster & Builder #12

Plan an un-birthday party for a family member. Then, invite them to the party and celebrate. As a reminder, an un-birthday is any day that does not fall on one's actual birthday. The Mad Hatter and March Hare started this tradition in the book, *Alice in Wonderland*.

Buster & Builder #13

If an un-birthday party is a celebration that falls on any day except one's actual birthday, then an unValentine's is an expression of love that falls on any day except Valentine's Day. Create unValentine's Day cards, or plan an unValentine's Day party, letting important people in your life know how much you care about them.

Buster & Builder #14

Bounce a balloon in the air 100 times without letting it touch the floor. If this is too easy, try it a second time without using your hands.

Buster & Builder #15

Learn a new magic trick. Practice it and demonstrate it to each family member in your home.

Buster & Builder #16

Write a poem about things you like to do. Recite it over tonight's dinner.

Buster & Builder #17

Build an enormous Lego castle. See if you can include every Lego you own.

Buster & Builder #18

Grab your comb, brush, chenille stems, and anything else needed to give yourself a wild and crazy new hairdo.

Buster & Builder #19

Organize a movie night. Create your own movie tickets, make popcorn, and transform your family room into a theatre. For added fun, convert a large cardboard box into a car and make it a drive-in movie.

Buster & Builder #20

Create an obstacle course using items you have in your home. Time yourself going through it. Then go through a second time, trying to beat your previous time.

Buster & Builder #21

Read a book for at least fifteen minutes.

Buster & Builder #22

Make a flipbook, where a stick figure or other objects move as you riffle through the pages.

Buster & Builder #23

Learn to fold a new origami creation.

Buster & Builder #24

Create your own miniature-golf course using items you have around your home.

Buster & Builder #25

Go for a bike ride.

Buster & Builder #26

Practice riding your bike without using your hands.

Buster & Builder #27

Make puppets out of socks or paper bags. Then put on a show.

Buster & Builder #28

Create an outdoor bowling game using items you have around the home.

Buster & Builder #29

Build a sandcastle. Better yet, during winter, transform your garage or basement into a beach paradise. Use your sandbox, plastic kid pool, beach toys, umbrella, space heater, and any other supplies you have. Jenny's dad did this for her when she was a child, and Jenny continues to share this happy memory to this day!

Buster & Builder #30

Play hopscotch. Use sidewalk chalk to create a traditional hopscotch board. Then, after a few games, add boxes to create your own design.

Buster & Builder #31

Prepare for the next American Idol competition. Select your song, practice it, and come prepared to perform at dinner.

Buster & Builder #32

Learn to do a handstand or a cartwheel. If you already know how to do these, then put together a gymnastic routine.

Buster & Builder #33

Get in costume and act out a play. You can recruit friends to help you or do it all yourself.

Buster & Builder #34

Do a puzzle. Then carefully turn the puzzle over and write a secret message on the back. Break the puzzle apart and give it to a friend. He or she will need to complete the puzzle to read your message.

Buster & Builder #35

Use your art supplies to create an original board game. Then teach it to family and friends.

Buster & Builder #36

Play a board game.

Buster & Builder #37

Do mazes or dot-to-dot puzzles. You can find a book you already own or find free printable worksheets online.

Buster & Builder #38

Draw your own book of mazes. For added fun, make copies and time how long it takes each family member to complete them.

Buster & Builder #39

Draw your own book of dot-to-dot puzzles.

Buster & Builder #40

Use your art supplies and items from home to build a boat that floats. Take it to a pond, lake, or bathtub to confirm it works. For added fun, build sailboats with your family and race them across a small pool.

Buster & Builder #41

Jump rope.

Buster & Builder #42

Swing.

Buster & Builder #43

Make your own joke book filled with your favorite jokes.

Buster & Builder #44

Create an inspirational poster to hang on your wall.

Buster & Builder #45

Create a book listing people and things you are grateful to have in your life. Strive to reach at least 100 reasons you are thankful.

Buster & Builder #46

Create your own knock-knock jokes–the sillier, the better.

Buster & Builder #47

Select a scripture or motivational quote that is meaningful to you and memorize it.

Buster & Builder #48

Make a robot out of your art supplies and other items you no longer use at home.

Buster & Builder #49

Make a nature book that identifies various types of animals, plants, rocks, and insects around your neighborhood.

Buster & Builder #50

Start a garden. If you don't have seeds, make a paper garden using your art supplies.

Buster & Builder #51

Make a treasure map, with clues leading to the treasure.

Buster & Builder #52

Paint with Q-tips instead of brushes.

Buster & Builder #53

Find three toys to donate to charity or someone in need.

Buster & Builder #54

Bake cookies and deliver them to a neighbor.

Buster & Builder #55

Make a list of five things you would like to know about your grandparents, then call and ask.

Buster & Builder #56

Help your parents clean whatever most needs to be cleaned in the home.

Buster & Builder #57

Create a nature art masterpiece. Use your paints, glue, rocks, leaves, flowers, and other objects you find outside.

Buster & Builder #58

Have a thumb war with everyone in your home. Be sure to create a special super-hero costume for your thumb first.

Buster & Builder #59

Play a game of tic-tac-toe. For added fun, build a giant board on the carpet. Use masking tape to create the board and paper plates with Xs and Os drawn on the back.

Buster & Builder #60

Design a Frisbee-golf course outside. Then play a game of Frisbee golf.

Buster & Builder #61

Build a lemonade stand and have a sale.

Buster & Builder #62

Make wind chimes using only art supplies and items gathered from around your home.

Buster & Builder #63

Pretend you are a professional reporter and interview a family member. Write out the questions you will ask, conduct your interview, and give a report of what you learned over dinner.

Buster & Builder #64

Make a playdough zoo.

Buster & Builder #65

Send an email to your grandparents. Ask them what they did when they were bored as kids.

Buster & Builder #66

Water the outdoor plants.

Buster & Builder #67

Build a birdhouse using items you already have at home.

Buster & Builder #68

Build a secret fort outdoors.

Buster & Builder #69

Play a game of marbles.

Buster & Builder #70

Play a game of hangman.

Buster & Builder #71

Record a movie on your parent's smartphone and send it to your grandparents. For bonus points, ask your grandparents to send a movie back.

If you carry your childhood with you,
you never become older.
~ Tom Stoppard

Buster & Builder #72

Create an indoor scavenger hunt with clues to a homemade prize.

Buster & Builder #73

Make your own finger puppets and put on a show.

Buster & Builder #74

Ask a family member what their favorite Bible story is. Then look up the story and read it.

Buster & Builder #75

Put on a lip-sync show that includes all of your favorite songs. For an added challenge, also include your parents' and grandparents' favorite songs.

Buster & Builder #76

Put on a dance show.

Buster & Builder #77

Play hackysack with a friend. If you are alone, then set a new personal hackysack record for the most touches without the ball falling to the ground.

Buster & Builder #78

Build a rubber-band shooting range out of Legos, toilet paper tubes, and other items from around your home. Then engage in target practice.

Buster & Builder #79

Write the first chapter of your new book. Then share it with your family over dinner.

Buster & Builder #80

Read a chapter in a nonfiction book that your parents choose for you.

Buster & Builder #81

Read a comic book, or better yet, create your own comic book or comic strip.

Buster & Builder #82

Draw plans depicting how you would like to reorganize your room.

Buster & Builder #83

Create a stuffed animal zoo. Give your family a tour. For bonus points, create an informational brochure and a map.

Buster & Builder #84

Build a kite using only items you already have at home. Be sure to test it.

Buster & Builder #85

Create your own jigsaw puzzle out of construction paper or cardboard.

Buster & Builder #86

Journal about the happiest memory you can recall.

Buster & Builder #87

Have a paper airplane race.

Buster & Builder #88

Make a friendship bracelet and give it to a friend.

Buster & Builder #89

For girls, dress up as Cinderella and sweep the kitchen floors.

Buster & Builder #90

Sweep the patios. Pretend you are an undercover spy, using sweeping as a cover to gather top-secret information.

Buster & Builder #91

Create a favorite fairytale scene in a cardboard box by using your art supplies and toys.

Buster & Builder #92

Practice with a yo-yo and learn a trick.

Buster & Builder #93

Have an indoor snowball fight using crumpled-up newspaper in place of snowballs. Be sure to build your fort first.

Buster & Builder #94

Set the table for dinner. Get extra fancy by making place cards for everyone.

Buster & Builder #95

Create dinner place cards that tell each family member something you like about him or her.

Buster & Builder #96

Look at a cookbook and find something that you would like to learn how to cook. Then make a grocery list of the ingredients you will need.

Buster & Builder #97

Play Jacks.

Buster & Builder #98

Vacuum the family room.

Buster & Builder #99

Listen to a chapter from an audiobook

Buster & Builder #100

Help fold laundry, or better yet, have a family laundry-folding day. Be sure to turn up the music!

Buster & Builder #101

Play store. Create your own play money and items to sell.

Buster & Builder #102

Have an indoor Nerf-gun fight. This is a new family favorite in our home.

Buster & Builder #103

Build an epic sculpture using only marshmallows and toothpicks.

Buster & Builder #104

Offer to do chores for a neighbor who could use an extra hand.

Buster & Builder #105

Practice skipping a bar on the monkey bars. Then see how many you can skip.

Buster & Builder #106

Roller-skate or rollerblade. Learn to skate backward too.

Buster & Builder #107

Create a mosaic out of glue and torn pieces of construction paper.

Buster & Builder #108

Volunteer in the church nursery for a day.

Buster & Builder #109

Create your own address book. Then ask your friends for their addresses so you can add them to your book.

Buster & Builder #110

Create a get-well card and send it to someone you know who is ill.

Buster & Builder #111

Create an "I-miss-you" card and send it to someone you have not seen for a while.

Buster & Builder #112

Create and send a thank-you card to someone you need to thank.

Buster & Builder #113

Make a paper chain. Use it to decorate your room or simply see how long you can make it.

Buster & Builder #114

Look through one of your parents' old photo albums—preferably one before you were born. Then come up with three questions you want to ask your parents based on the pictures in the album.

Buster & Builder #115

Draw the blueprints to a brand new invention. The only requirement is that whatever you design cannot currently exist.

Buster & Builder #116

Turn yourself into a superhero. Create your costume and invent a story about how you use your powers to make the world a better place.

Buster & Builder #117

Write and illustrate a children's book.

Buster & Builder #118

Build an indoor fort out of couch cushions and bed sheets.

Buster & Builder #119

Dip long strands of colorful yarn into Elmer's glue. Carefully add the sticky mess to a piece of construction paper or to an inflated balloon to make a yarn-art masterpiece.

Buster & Builder #120

Create your own sticker book. Use a sheet of wax paper for some of the pages so you can remove and share your stickers.

Buster & Builder #121

Create an indoor bowling alley. Use empty decorated 2-liter pop bottles for the pins and bowl with a soccer ball. Then invite your family to a bowling competition.

Buster & Builder #122

Find and decorate a pet rock. Then make a leash and take your pet for a walk.

Buster & Builder #123

Publish a family newspaper. Report on recent and upcoming family events. Then post your paper on the refrigerator or another high-traffic area in the home.

Buster & Builder #124

Have a tea party. Then invite your friends. Real, imaginary, and stuffed animal friends are all welcome.

Buster & Builder #125

Find costumes, dress up in funny clothes, and have a photo shoot.

Buster & Builder #126

Assign everyone in your family a superhero identity. Then draw a picture of how they would look in full superhero attire.

Buster & Builder #127

Build your own piñata. Combine one cup of water and two cups of flour. Mix well. Inflate a balloon, and tear apart thin strips of newspaper. Completely cover the newspaper strips in the water and flour concoction. Place them on the inflated balloon, one at a time, until fully covered. Once this dries, paint your piñata.

Buster & Builder #128

Plan a ten-minute exercise routine consisting of pushups, sit-ups, jumping jacks, and whatever other exercises you want to add. Then put your plan into action.

Buster & Builder #129

Practice hula-hooping or teach yourself a new hula-hoop trick.

Buster & Builder #130

Carve a figurine using a butter knife and a bar of soap.

<u>Buster & Builder #131</u>

Create your own book of boredom busters and creativity builders. Fill it with your creative ideas, and be sure to include plenty of pictures.

Living Creatively

Today, Jenny and I are striving to live what we teach. In June 2017, our family relocated from sunny San Diego, California, to a small town in Minnesota. Initially, the two of us were a little uneasy about how the move would affect our kids. Fortunately, there was no need to fear. Our family has discovered that the slower pace of small-town life suits us well.

Our children refer to our much larger backyard as "the park," and love spending the long, lazy summer days outdoors. Neighbors frequently stop by just to say hi, and when little Addison got sick, they brought treats and let us know that our family was in their prayers. I am also exceedingly happy to report that, after a few days in the hospital, little Addison has fully recovered.

This is not to suggest that life is perfect. Like all families, we continue to have challenges. Life is, however, remarkably good. While Jenny and I are not anti-television, nor have we declared war on electronics, somehow these things seem less important than ever before.

Both Jenny and I have grown through this process of helping our children rediscover the simple joys of life. Each of us has discovered that a balanced approach is best. I, Jed, have learned that the girls will not die of boredom when the electronics are turned off. I am also learning that I do not need to keep our kids continually entertained. As it turns out, with a little prompting, they are fully capable of having hours upon hours of fun on their own.

Jenny, on the other hand, has eased up when it comes to electronic devices. She is no longer concerned that the occasional television binge will ruin the girls' eyes or that a goofy show will abruptly transform them into mindless zombies. In short, the two of us balance each other out nicely.

Every family is different, and there is no one right way to do things. Each family must decide what works best for their unique style and culture. I hope that the creative ideas in this book, along with our family's own story, are helpful as you and your family navigate this road.

My most significant takeaway from this adventure is a better understanding of just how creative our children can be. I wish you many boredom-busting and highly creative experiences in the days ahead!

131
Stress Busters
and Mood Boosters
For Kids

How to help kids ease anxiety,
feel happy, and reach their goals!

Jed Jurchenko

www.CoffeeShopConversations.com

Get the Free Workbook!

Dive deeper with the *131 Stress Busters and Mood Boosters Workbook!*

This printable workbook is packed with activities that encourage kids to bust stress and boost their mood.

Activities Include:
- Conversation Cards
- Self-Regulation Word Searches
- Coping Skills Fortuneteller Activity
- Self-Talk Mazes and more

Download your free workbook at:
www.CoffeeShopConversations.com/BustStress

Dedication

Dedicated to parents, stepparents, foster parents, teachers, mentors, and coaches who tirelessly build into the lives of kids.

Dedicated to children and tweens who are in the process of learning how to bust stress and boost their mood as they patiently pursue their goals.

Dedicated to my own children, Mackenzie, Brooklyn, Addison, and Emmalynn. Your love for life is contagious! May your adventuresome spirit and creativity continue to grow.

131 Stress Busters and mood Boosters for Kids

👍👍👍

The Power of Self-Regulation

Children who can self-regulate have higher odds of excelling virtually everywhere. Parents who teach their kids to bust stress, boost their mood, and persistently press forward toward their goals not only pass on an invaluable skill but also equip their children to win at life. Thanks to Professor Walter Mischel and his team of Stanford University graduate students, there is ample evidence supporting this.

In the 1960s, Professor Mischel began researching how preschoolers manage stress. He created an experiment that took place in an area dubbed *The Surprise Room,* and data was collected from over six hundred four-, five-, and six-year-old children. Furnished with only a table and chair (and equipped with a panel of two-way glass to conceal the presence of the research team), *The Surprise Room* was intentionally distraction free.

In this space, Walter's tiny participants played a game that put their ability to self-regulate to the test. One by one, each child was ushered into the room, seated at the table, and asked to select a small treat. Because children often chose a marshmallow, the experiment eventually became known as *The Marshmallow Experiment*.

Each child was offered a simple choice. He or she could devour a single marshmallow now or enjoy two marshmallows later. The only catch was the child would have to wait an entire fifteen minutes to receive the additional reward. The researcher then placed the marshmallow on the table and exited the room.

Having the sweet indulgence within arm's reach created a stressful situation for the child and ideal conditions for Walter's research. Could these kids defend against temptation? What skills would they use to resist the enticing treats? This is precisely what Walter and his team wanted to know.

As you might imagine, some children gulped down the marshmallow at once.

Others held out for a few minutes before relenting. Out of the children who attempted to wait, only one in three managed to hold out the entire fifteen minutes. Although the study itself is fascinating, the research gathered over the following decades is what makes this experiment truly extraordinary. Over the next forty years, Walter's team remained in contact with their original participants, amassing as much information about their lives as possible.

The results are astounding. Children who waited to eat the marshmallow as preschoolers grew up to have "higher SAT scores, lower levels of substance abuse, a lower likelihood of obesity, better responses to stress, better social skills as reported by their parents, and generally better scores in a range of other life measures."[1] This includes higher self-reported levels of happiness, fewer instances of divorce, and higher rates of relationship satisfaction. In short, children who waited to eat the marshmallow were winning at life!

Today, Walter's work is highly regarded. It is taught in psychology courses and is the subject of popular Ted Talks, books, and internet articles. Duplicate experiments have even been uploaded to YouTube.[2] Undoubtedly, this simple test resonates with people profoundly.

Avoiding Life's Marshmallows

So why are adults attracted to this study like a child to a marshmallow? I believe it is because nearly everyone can relate to the struggles of waiting and to the ecstasy of reaching one's goal. At first glance, connecting adult success with a single childhood decision not to gulp down a marshmallow may seem overly simplistic. However, upon closer examination, this correlation makes sense.

Obviously, *The Marshmallow Experiment* is not about the marshmallow. Children who waited to eat the treat went on to excel, not due to their capacity to avoid sugar but because of their ability to assert effortful control over their lives. In other words, when these kids needed to delay gratification to reach their objective, they could. Whether this quality is called effortful control, patient persistence, grit, or self-regulation, the same set of skills applies. The common factors include:

1. Being able to reduce one's level of stress so as not to be overwhelmed by frustrations.

2. The ability to make oneself reasonably happy in the moment.

3. The capacity to keep going until the goal is attained.

Everyday Marshmallows

To better understand the significance of these skills, let's examine some examples of real-life marshmallows that kids face:

- Watching television instead of completing chores.

- Guzzling soda and junk foods to the detriment of a balanced diet.

- Playing video games and electronics instead of studying for a test.

- Chatting with friends late into the evening as opposed to getting a full night's rest.

- Avoiding a daily regimen of brushing and flossing because it feels like too much work.

- Refusing to share one's toys with friends because this is more appealing at the moment.

These common childhood traps shed light on why self-regulation matters. Imagine how much better life could be for your child if he or she were able to remain reasonably content while completing difficult but important tasks.

Marshmallow-avoiding Adults

The Marshmallow Study reveals that marshmallow-resisting children grow up to become marshmallow-resisting adults. Self-regulation is like riding a bike. Although challenging at first, once mastered, the ability sticks for life.

As children transition into adulthood, the capacity to manage negative emotions in a positive way becomes even more advantageous. Illustrations of this include the self-regulating employee who puts personal drama on pause so he can fully engage at work. This makes it far more likely that he will receive a raise. Self-regulated couples set aside their differences to connect, which increases their odds of a happy, healthy, lasting relationship. One example of this is the husband who chooses to record a sporting event and attend the opera with his wife, even though he does not particularly enjoy opera. This wise husband knows that making time for his spouse is far more important than any game.

Do you get the picture? The ability to remain positive while steadily pursuing one's aspirations makes all the difference. The next logical question is "How do parents nurture this quality in their kids?" or more playfully stated, "How do parents help children circumvent life's marshmallows?"

Mastering the Art of Coping

Marshmallow-avoiding children are not born with magical abilities. In fact, it is fascinating to note that many of the skills observed by Walter and his team were unsophisticated and even downright gross. Yet, the strategies worked.

So how did these future successes of the world make waiting easier? They distracted themselves by sticking their fingers in their nose, mouth, and ears, exploring every orifice of their face—disgusting for sure! They sat on their hands, rendering themselves physically incapable of yielding to temptation—a simple strategy that also happened to be exactly what that child needed in the moment. Other children hummed, sang, distracted themselves with finger play, pushed the delicacy away, attempted to fall asleep, covered their eyes, and turned their back toward the treat.

Avoiding marshmallows is not rocket science. Basic stress-management skills allowed these children to reach their goal, which makes me wonder if equipping children with the skills to succeed might be easier than we think.

Therapists refer to these strategies as coping skills. All successful people, regardless of their age, title, or stage of life, have an arsenal of positive coping skills at their disposal. However, the application of these skills often looks quite different. For instance, the marathon runner who pushes through the pain by mentally repeating, *Running is simply placing one foot in front of the other,* is employing a positive coping skill to finish the race. The department store employee who takes a deep breath, smiles, and says, "Yes, I can see you are frustrated, and I will do my best to help," when confronted by an irate customer, is also using a healthy coping skill.

On a personal level, there are moments when writing is so exasperating that tossing my laptop off the balcony in a fit of frustration would feel especially gratifying. However, when I instead choose to pause for a break by walking to the refrigerator, pouring a cold glass of water, and then returning to the task at hand, I too am putting coping skills to work.

Equipping Children to Win

This book provides an arsenal of coping skills to help children bust stress, boost their mood, and patiently pursue their goals. When practiced consistently, this pattern leads to success. And it works in virtually every area of life! Because coping skills develop over time, teaching, modeling, and practicing these skills with your kids on a consistent basis is especially important. In short, taking action is far more valuable than merely knowing what one should do.

In the pages ahead, you will find 131 stress-busting, mood-boosting coping skills. Your job is to teach them to your children and to reinforce them at every opportunity you get. Doing this will embed these skills in your child's memory and make them his or her automatic response to stress. The best time to teach these coping skills is now. Fortunately, one is never too young or too old to implement the ideas in this book.

Helping Kids Cope

From the moment a child is born, parents help their kids learn how to cope. A crying baby, who is nursed, changed, and gently soothed to sleep, is taught to seek support from others—a skill that will serve him well for the rest of his life. As children mature, they develop the ability to apply increasingly complex skills, such as stacking coping skills together. This strategy is expanded upon in later chapters.

My simple definition of a coping skill is *any healthy strategy that allows a child to feel good enough to persist.* I like the phrase "good enough," because it highlights a balanced approach. Contrary to what some self-help gurus suggest, it is not necessary to feel elated all the time. This would be exhausting. Instead, the aim is to prevent negative emotions from taking over. Sometimes life is hard. No skills will change this. The ideas in this book do, however, assist children in persisting through challenges without becoming overwhelmed in the process.

Eustress and Distress

Cars need oil changes, computers require restarts, and the human body must have rest. This is true even during happy times. According to psychology, there are two types of stress. Distresses are events that feel bad. Common childhood distresses include failing a test, losing a longstanding friendship, and completing chores at home. However, stress also comes in sneakier forms. *Eustress* is a term that describes positive life events that contribute to stress buildup. For adults, getting married, buying a house, or receiving a promotion at work are all eustress events, as these activities are amazing and emotionally taxing at the same time.

For children, moving to a new home (even if the new one is nicer), switching schools, making new friends, becoming the star player on a sports team, and reaching major milestones contribute to eustress buildup. Stressors, both good and bad, big and small, are everywhere and frequently go unnoticed. Because stress is cumulative, it has a knack of sneaking up and overwhelming kids.

Kids, Stress, and Gunpowder

Stress is like a barrel of gunpowder. When kids stuff stress inside, it accumulates and packs tight. Eventually, a tiny upset sparks an immense explosion. The child's outburst might manifest in a fit of anger, a river of tears, or in the child giving up. Whenever an emotional outburst is far greater than the situation warrants, stress buildup is usually involved.

Fortunately, self-regulation skills allow children to release their gunpowder-like stress and avoid the explosion. Using coping skills throughout the day is similar to sprinkling a barrel of gunpowder over a large parking lot. When ignited, instead of a "BOOM," there is only a sizzle and a "poof." No damage is done because the stress was released over time.

Rest for Success

Life sends ongoing barrages of stressors our kid's way. Because of this, it is essential that children learn to establish consistent rhythms of rest. When your child's first reaction to a negative event is to take a deep breath and remind herself she is capable of handling the difficulty, then you have done your job well.

Recently a manager friend expressed her disappointment at the number of job applicants who missed their interviews. She remarked, "Sometimes I think 50 percent of success comes from just showing up." I would agree and expand on this wisdom. In my opinion, roughly 90 percent of success results from showing up consistently and completing the task at hand while maintaining a positive attitude in the process.

Although this percentage is only an assumption, I think most people will agree. The ability to regulate one's emotions and press forward until a goal is achieved is the most basic recipe for success. This is what allowed a handful of preschoolers to avoid eating the marshmallow, and according to the research, it is what will allow your child to triumph in nearly every area of life.

Why Coping Skills Work

Coping skills prevent kids from losing their minds and behaving like animals. Without them, children act impulsively, saying things they do not mean and hurting those they love. While this may sound like an odd statement, it is based on biological research. Let me further explain with a story.

It was the end of a gorgeous fall day. The sun was setting as our family traveled home from our annual apple-picking excursion in the quaint town of Julian. Little did we know that we had one more adventure in store. I was behind the wheel of our family's white minivan. My wife, Jenny, sat next to me, chatting about the events of the day, while our four children happily hunkered down with books and movies in the back.

After traversing a bend in the road, I spotted a fully-grown mountain lion peering out from the woods. In San Diego, a mountain lion sighting is a rare occurrence, so my initial reaction was excitement.

However, as I enthusiastically encouraged my family to look out the windows, something alarming occurred. The beast bolted into the road, froze in the center of our lane, and gave us an icy glare.

A flood of questions whirled through my mind. *If I slam on the breaks, will I be rear-ended by the car behind us? Is it safe to stop this close to a mountain lion? Will my family be injured if our vehicle collides with the beast?*

The next few seconds felt like an eternity. Lacking clear direction, I eased my foot on the breaks—slowing but not stopping our vehicle—and hoped for the best. Sensing the oncoming danger, the mountain lion scrambled into the woods. Regrettably, he was not quite fast enough. Our slowing minivan gingerly clipped his hindquarters as he sped away. Luckily, no lasting damage was done. However, that mountain lion will undoubtedly think twice before attempting to stare down another vehicle.

Panic-button Problems

I share this story because it illustrates how a tiny part of the brain can hijack one's ability to think critically. So why did that mountain lion unexpectedly bolt into the road? According to psychology, this animal took flight, froze, prepared to fight, and then took flight again for the same reason people do. His amygdala hijacked his brain. The amygdala is the brain's crude emergency response system that can be both a help and a hindrance. In other words, everyone has panic-button problems.

When people are triggered, similar to a spooked mountain lion, they act in irrationally impulsive ways. The amygdala is what causes a couple who is deeply in love to argue bitterly, to the point of scarring their relationship for life. It is why children break their favorite toys during temper tantrums and drop out of activities they love after experiencing a minor setback.

This tiny, almond-shaped portion of the brain is responsible for the fight, flight, or freeze reactions in our bodies. Although these primal instincts are a lifesaver in genuine emergencies, they stir up chaos during false alarms. To understand how this works, picture the amygdala and the frontal cortex — or the critical thinking part of the brain—connected by a switch. When one turns on, the other turns off. This means that when the amygdala activates, clear and rational thinking is nearly impossible.

To drive this point home, one of my favorite college professors refers to the amygdala as "Amy G. Dala." This personification keenly portrays the hijacking power of this tiny mass of gray matter. Amy G. is highly emotional. She does not think but simply acts. Sensing danger as our vehicle approached, Amy G. ordered the mountain lion to take flight. Unfortunately, Amy G. is fickle. She quickly changed her mind, deciding that freezing then fighting would be better. Fortunately, before a head-on collision ensued, Amy G. commanded the mountain lion to resume its flight.

As one would expect, Amy G. wreaks havoc when critical thinking is required. Relationships are where she does her most damage. Close connections are something that Amy G. knows little about. Unfortunately, this does not deter her from getting involved, which is precisely why equipping kids with tools to avert Amy G.'s influence is so important.

Amy G. and Your Child

In a crisis, such as a fire, burglary, or earthquake, Amy G. passionately strives to keep children safe. She pushes them to run, take cover, hide, and fight back. While this can be a good thing, Amy G.'s trigger-happy nature is not. Her motto is "better safe than sorry," and she is ready to shut down a child's frontal cortex at the first sign of danger.

Sadly, Amy G. does not recognize the seriousness of the consequences that result. Children who are emotionally triggered will act in ways that are out of character. For instance, a typically gentle child may become verbally aggressive, rageful, or violent. A normally caring individual might shut down, isolate, or boldly proclaim that he or she no longer cares at all. When a rational child acts recklessly during emotionally charged circumstances, Amy G. is usually involved.

Soothing Amy G.

The first reason the strategies in this book work is because they soothe Amy G. When a child notices feelings of panic welling up inside and pauses to take a deep breath, the amygdala relaxes. This allows the frontal cortex to remain in control, which drastically increases the odds of a positive outcome.

The amygdala is sometimes referred to as "the reptilian brain," and it is easy to see why. Even lizards know how to fight, freeze, and take flight. A basic key to success is continually thinking at a higher level than a reptile. Children who are able to prevent Amy G. from taking charge of non-emergency situations have fewer temper outbursts, emotional shutdowns, and moments of despair. Thus, they are better equipped to handle life.

Draining Toxic Stress

A second reason the strategies in this book work is because they alleviate stress before it turns toxic. Contrary to popular belief, not all stress is bad. Because of this, the goal is not to eliminate stress but to equip kids with tools for managing it in healthy ways.

Interestingly, there are three different types of stress. The first is healthy stress, a powerful motivator that leads to mastering new skills, achieving goals, and seeking help from others. Healthy stress is beneficial because a completely stress-free life would also be an unmotivated life. From a practical standpoint, healthy stress pushes children to complete homework assignments, practice before a big game, and act responsibly at home. In limited doses, stress provides children with an extra push to complete difficult but essential tasks.

The second level of stress is tolerable stress. Tolerable stress is an increasing pressure that leads to anxiety. A child who wakes up in a panic because he did not practice the school presentation due that day will experience tolerable stress. Although this type of stress feels bad, it does not cause lasting damage.

The final and most severe level of stress is toxic stress. Toxic stress results from prolonged activation of the amygdala. According to neuroscience, a continually heightened state of arousal will eventually alter the brain's architecture. In other words, toxic stress causes the amygdala to take over. This leads to a diminished capacity for critical thinking that becomes the new norm.

Toxic Stress and Mental Illness

With this in mind, it is not surprising to learn that toxic stress leads to mental illness. According to the diathesis-stress model of mental illness, it is possible for people to drive themselves crazy — literally! The term *diathesis* refers to a genetic propensity for mental illness present in everyone. Some children are especially susceptible to depression. Others are more prone to anxiety, oppositional defiant disorders, schizophrenia, or bipolar disorder. When a person's level of stress elevates above the threshold that they can bear, the symptoms of mental illness kick in, amplifying with increased and prolonged exposure.

Eliminating Toxic Build-up

Stress is cumulative. What begins as tolerable stress can turn toxic. Dealing with toxic stress is not this book's goal, as this is best accomplished under the guidance of a skilled therapist. Instead, the aim is to help children prevent healthy stress and tolerable stress from reaching toxic levels.

One way stress turns toxic is when children hone-in on their worries. This causes problems to feel bigger than they truly are and leads to feeling worse. Albert Ellis, the founder of Rational Emotive Behavioral Therapy, refers to this as *awfulizing* and *catastrophizing*.

Poor coping also increases the toxicity of stress. For instance, eating an entire pan of brownies produces an initial high that ends in a new low once the sugar hangover kicks in. The next chapter provides positive alternative strategies that help kids avoid these toxic traps.

Bursting the Happiness Myth

Finally, the strategies in this book help children feel happier. The idea that self-care is selfish is a myth. Children who practice healthy self-care not only boost their mood, they also provide an amazing gift to others. Moods are highly contagious, and when your child is happy, everyone they meet will share in this joy. If you doubt this, the next time a baby smiles at you, I challenge you to try not smiling back. Thanks to *mirror neurons*, this is practically impossible.

Let me further explain. In the early 1990s, a team of Italian researchers discovered mirror neurons, or neurons that fire when one human being detects an emotion in another. This means that the act of observing someone else smile actually causes the observer to feel happier. People literally share in the joy of others. For this reason, when children attend to their happiness needs, they lift the moods of everyone they meet.

Why Happiness Matters

One of my favorite quotes comes from Ray Tucker. Ray states, "There are two types of leaders, those who generate energy and those who consume energy. Be a leader who generates energy." To fit with the theme of this book, I would tweak this to proclaim, "There are two types of kids, those who spread happiness and those who consume happiness. Help your kids to bust stress, boost their mood, and spread joy to everyone they meet!" Parents who help their children accomplish this endow them with an extraordinary skill that benefits them for the rest of their life!

Now, that we have examined how these stress-busting and mood-boosting skills work, it is time to take action. I wish you and your kids much success as you begin the journey ahead.

131

Stress Busters
and Mood Boosters

You're braver than you believe,
and stronger than you seem,
and smarter than you think.

~Christopher Robin

Courage is not the absence of fear,
but doing something in spite of fear.

~Unknown

Don't underestimate the value
of doing nothing, of just going along,
listening to all the things you can't hear,
and not bothering.

~Winnie the Pooh

Breathe Deeply

"Take a deep breath, and calm down." You have likely heard this advice before and, perhaps, have even given it yourself. Even so, this simple strategy is worth repeating, because breathing deeply works. Whether you are a 2-year-old or 102, filling your lungs to capacity then gradually releasing the air is a foundational way of preventing an amygdala hijacking from occurring.

I have taught this skill to adults as part of a fifty-two-week domestic violence offenders program. I have also used a bubble-wand and a pinwheel to practice this skill with toddlers. So why does this strategy work? Taking a deep breath oxygenates the brain, slows the body down, and provides additional time for children to think.

When kids are upset, quick and shallow breathing is the norm. This increases anxiety and prepares the body to react. I sometimes tell the impulsive teenagers I see, "It's awesome that we get to meet now before any lasting damage is done. Our goal is to help you to avoid bigger mistakes in the future and the consequences that come with them."

The first six strategies in this book help kids to improve their mood by taking slow, deep breaths. Although this skill is simple, it is surprisingly potent. Thus, encouraging kids to practice taking deep breaths, to the point it becomes second nature, is highly recommended.

Buster & Booster #1

Take a big, deep breath.

> Inhale through your nose and exhale through your mouth. When kids find themselves amid tense situations, this is also the perfect time for them to step away and reorient before deciding what to do next.

Buster & Booster #2

Blow a pinwheel, and see how long you can keep the wheel spinning.

Buster & Booster #3

Blow bubbles.

Buster & Booster #4

Blow feathers.

> Kids can cup their hands together and blow the feathers out or propel a single feather across a tabletop.

Buster & Booster #5

Take elephant breaths.

> Stand with your feet apart, body bent slightly forward, and arms dangling in front of you like an elephant's trunk. Slowly breathe in through your nose. As you do, raise your body and extend your arms until you are standing straight, with your arms fully raised above your head. As you exhale through your mouth, gradually return to your original position.

Buster & Booster #6

Go for a swim.

> Not only is swimming excellent exercise but it is also a fantastic way for kids to learn how to control their breathing.

Be Fully Present

According to *The Worry Cure*, worrying is normal. In fact, worrying is so common that roughly 35 percent of people engage in it daily.[3] However, because 85 percent of the things people worry about never happen, worrying is mostly worthless. More importantly, studies reveal that when bad things do ensue, 79 percent of the time they are not as bad as expected, or the situation is managed better than anticipated. This means that 97 percent of the time, worry only creates unnecessary misery.

When children worry, they are physically secure, but their mind becomes trapped in a negative past or future event. It is important to note there is nothing wrong with some anxiety. In limited doses, this is a normal, healthy, and motivating emotion. However, when children get stuck in worry, the resulting anxiety can become debilitating.

This next set of stress busters and mood boosters helps children return their focus to the present. After all, this is the only place they can be truly happy. Also, since the majority of what kids worry about never transpires, worrying is simply not worth the effort.

Buster & Booster #7

Use the 5-4-3-2-1 technique to return to the present moment.

> Kids can do this by identifying five things they see, four things they hear, three things they feel (e.g., the solid ground beneath their feet, the soft clothes they are wearing, the wind against their face), two things they smell, and one thing they taste.

Buster & Booster #8

Splash cool water on your face.

> The slight change in temperature, coupled with the sensory experience, helps children return to the here and now.

Buster & Booster #9

Squeeze an ice cube.

This coping skill packs a double-whammy, as the squeezing of the fist and the cold of the ice take the focus away from problems and on to the present moment.

Buster & Booster #10

Sit with the pain and experience it fully.

Strong emotions do not last forever, and sometimes the quickest way to the other side is straight through. Because our emotional response system is not designed to remain under duress for long, when a child sits with the pain, the intensity of the feelings will dissipate. This tool is not appropriate for every child, but under the right circumstances, it can work well.

Buster & Booster #11

Draw a picture of your anger, fear, sadness, or frustration.

This helps children to understand better what they are feeling. Then talk about the picture, listen empathetically, and assure your child that he or she is safe at this moment.

Buster & Booster #12

Schedule a time to be upset later.

> For example, schedule ten minutes of worry at 5 p.m. When the set time rolls around, some kids will find they no longer need it. Other children will want to stick to the schedule. In this case, children discover they have some ability to manage their emotions.

Buster & Booster #13

Allow yourself five minutes to be upset now.

> This strategy is perfect for children who are unable to wait. Simply set a timer and allow your child time to vent. Listen empathetically. Provide comfort in the moment. Then, after the timer dings, shift into the present moment, where life is good. This is another excellent way to help children increase their emotional control.

Change Your Temperature

Every year, I teach a general psychology class where the textbook teaches that temperature influences mood.[4] Did you know that more acts of violence occur during the heat of the summer months? Fortunately, a chilly drink or cool shower can help soothe anger on a sweltering day.

Similarly, a warm bath or a cozy drink on a frosty day can cause the world to feel brighter. This next set of stress busters and mood boosters demonstrates how to use changes in temperature to help your child self-regulate.

Buster & Booster #14

Sip a tall glass of ice water, lemonade, or another chilly drink.

Buster & Booster #15

Take a cool shower.

Buster & Booster #16

Place a cold washcloth on your forehead.

Buster & Booster #17

Sip hot tea, apple cider, or cocoa.

Buster & Booster #18

Take a warm bath.

> Add bubbles or a few drops of lavender oil for an additional calming effect.

Act Happy

An easy way for a child to feel happier is to act happier. Psychology teaches that we are biopsychosocial beings. This complex term describes how biology, psychology, and social interactions intertwine to influence moods and actions. *Biology* refers to the chemical makeup of our physical bodies. *Psychology* encompasses our thoughts and mental process, and the word *social* describes our interpersonal interactions.

The interconnectedness of my biology, psychology, and social relationships became clear during my junior year of high school. "Ok, let's try this again. I would like you to hold your hand palm-down and keep it as steady as possible." Yet it was no use. The sheet of notebook paper the doctor placed on my hand shook vehemently before drifting to the floor.

"Well, this explains a lot," the doctor exclaimed. "The reason you can't hold your hand still is because your heart is racing at 120 beats a minute. As you sit in my office, your heart is running a marathon."

I left the doctor's office diagnosed with Graves Disease, also known as a hyperactive thyroid. Somewhere toward the end of middle school, this tiny gland in my neck malfunctioned. This change in my biology created a chain reaction that also altered my thoughts and friendships.

I remember the balmy San Diego days where I would sweat profusely and struggle to stay focused in class, even though my peers seemed just fine. As you can imagine, my racing heart led to slipping grades, which caused me to think, *I am no good at school.* As a result, I adjusted my social interactions to fit my perceived identity by increasing my associations with slackers, underachievers, and the kids who didn't care. *After all,* I told myself, *this is where I belong.*

By the time my junior year in high school rolled around, I was a train wreck. Fortunately, a wise doctor helped me get back on track. All it took was a simple medication that brought my biology back into balance. Soon my grades improved, as did my self-esteem and the quality of my relationships.

I share this story because it demonstrates how one's biology, psychology, and social interactions all intertwine. It also illustrates how a boost in one area can elevate the others. Adults can use this knowledge to their advantage by helping children understand that happy kids act happy.

The physical act of smiling increases cheerful thoughts and the odds that someone else will smile back. These things work together to stir up genuine feelings of happiness. In other words, when children act the part, the feelings eventually follow. This next set of mood boosters helps children to feel happier by acting happier.

Buster & Booster #19

Smile. Better yet, look someone in the eyes and let a warm, gentle smile ease across your face.

According to psychology, the simple act of smiling makes one feel happier. I first discovered this principle in Dale Carnegie's classic, How to Win Friends and Influence People. Ever since, I have been pleasantly surprised at just how powerful this simple mood-boosting strategy is. Teach your kids to smile at family, friends, and peers they would like to meet. Not only will this brighten their day, chances are it will spread joy to those around them too.

Buster & Booster #20

Listen to positive, upbeat music.

Buster & Booster #21

Have a dance party.

This is a personal family favorite that has led to a multitude of happy memories in our home.

Buster & Booster #22

Watch a humorous movie or television show.

Buster & Booster #23

Read inspirational quotes.

Buster & Booster #24

Act like today will be amazing.

Buster & Booster #25

Look back to past successes.

> As you do, remind yourself that you
> succeeded once, and you can most certainly
> do it again!

Buster & Booster #26

Act like the most optimistic person you know.

> First, visualize the happiest person you know.
> Then, try to borrow this person's
> mannerisms, facial expressions, and attitude.
> Remember, happy people act happy. Go
> about your day as if you were in a positive
> mood, and the feelings will eventually
> follow.

Buster & Booster #27

Find an excuse to smile and laugh.

> Don't overthink this one. Any excuse will do.

Buster & Booster #28

Skip.

Draw Strength from Faith

In the Bible, many of the psalms begin in despair and end in joy. The reason for this is that David, who authored much of this book, knew how to draw strength from his faith.

As a psychology professor at a seminary, I have discovered that people regularly hold the misconception that psychology and faith mix about as well as orange juice and toothpaste or screen doors on a submarine. However, this is simply not the case. In fact, *Psychology*, a general psychology textbook authored by David Myers, lists nurturing one's spiritual self as a primary way to feel happier.

Myers states, "People active in faith communities report greater-than-average happiness and often cope well with crisis."[4] Faith brings hope. Because of this, helping kids draw strength from their faith is an excellent way to support them in busting stress and boosting their mood. The next section provides ideas for accomplishing this.

Buster & Booster #29

Pray.

Buster & Booster #30

Ask a pastor, lay minister, Sunday school teacher, or friend to pray for you.

Buster & Booster #31

Read a book of inspirational Scriptures.

Buster & Booster #32

Sing along to worship music in the car.

> My daughter, Addison, loves to rock out to "God's Not Dead," by The Newsboys, during our drive to school. She sings with so much enthusiasm that I look forward to this daily ritual. Moreover, a college student I know describes using worship music to transform high-stress, traffic-filled commutes into her "Jesus party time." After implementing this change, she reports arriving at work energized and refreshed.

Buster & Booster #33

Vent to God.

Many of the psalms begin in sorrow and end in joy. David was a master at venting his frustrations to his Creator and leaving problems in God's hands.

Buster & Booster #34

Read a kid's devotional book as a family.

Buster & Booster #35

Share with your child how you draw strength from your faith.

In 1 Corinthians 11:1, the apostle Paul writes, "Be imitators of me, just as I also am of Christ."[5] Wise adults teach children in a similar fashion. They live out their faith and inspire kids with their example.

Buster & Booster #36

Seek wisdom from a pastor, Sunday school teacher, or church leader.

One is never too young nor too old to seek advice from others.

Practice Gratitude

When kids practice gratitude, the world feels brighter. Gratitude not only boosts one's physical and mental health, but it also promotes an overall sense of wellbeing. In fact, gratitude's ability to lift one's spirits is so compelling that two researchers from the University of Miami, Robert Emmons and Michael McCullough, refer to it as "the forgotten factor in happiness research."[6]

During their study, Robert and Michael discovered that those who kept a weekly happiness journal exercised more often, had fewer adverse physical health symptoms, felt better about their lives, and were more optimistic than the control group (who only journaled about negative or neutral life events). In addition, those who practice gratitude daily are more likely to be a physical and emotional support to those in need.

Thus, gratitude is a powerful force that supercharges happiness. In regard to kids, it increases their energy, strengthens their relationships, and inspires them to support others. In a world bursting at the seams with entitled youth, many adults consider it a pleasure to be in the presence of a grateful adolescent.

However, helping children to appreciate the amazing things around them requires intentional effort. Gratitude is like a muscle; it develops with ongoing use. The next set of strategies hones in on ways adults can help kids bust stress and boost their mood by flexing their gratitude.

Buster & Booster #37

For a quick mood boost, list ten things you are thankful for right now.

> To make this even more powerful, encourage children to enlist the help of family members and create a gratitude journal of 100 items or more. Not only is this an exciting challenge, an extended gratitude list is a powerful resource that children can refer back to during discouraging moments in their lives.

Buster & Booster #38

Identify ten things that went well for you during the past week.

"What is going well?" This is one of my favorite questions to ask the kids I meet with. I am a firm believer that there are always positives in our children's lives. The trick is to find them. I have watched countless kids regain joy and rebuild momentum as they become aware of just how many positives they have.

Buster & Booster #39

Mail a thank-you card.

Buster & Booster #40

Send a thoughtful email or text with the goal of brightening someone else's day.

Buster & Booster #41

Thank your grandparents, teacher, or coach for building into your life.

When you do this, get as specific as possible. Tell them exactly what you appreciate and why it is so meaningful to you. This can be accomplished in a letter, through a phone call, or in person.

Get Active

According to psychology, aerobic exercise can alleviate mild depression and reduce anxiety. Of course, this is in addition to improving one's physical health and increasing mental clarity. Runners use the term *runner's high* to describe the pleasurable state that results from the body's release of natural endorphins. Moreover, being active is simply a whole lot of fun.

Personally, running is my cure for writer's block. This stress buster and mood booster always unlocks a vault of creativity. For some kids, being active comes naturally. Nevertheless, in today's high-tech world, others are sucked into the black hole of electronic devices. These kids will require extra motivation to get their bodies moving. This next section provides simple ways adults can inspire kids to increase their joy through physical activity.

Buster & Booster #42

Take a walk.

Buster & Booster #43

Go for a run.

Buster & Booster #44

Hike.

Buster & Booster #45

Throw a football.

Buster & Booster #46

Play basketball.

> If no one is around to play with you, see how many free throws you can make in two minutes, play a solo game of Around the World, or set up a dribbling obstacle course.

Buster & Booster #47

Do push-ups, crunches, lunges, or jumping jacks.

> Assist kids in putting together a simple exercise routine they can implement at home. Then encourage them to practice it three times a week or more.

Buster & Booster #48

Jump rope.

Try to get to 100 jumps without stopping.

Buster & Booster #49

Bounce on a trampoline.

Buster & Booster #50

Attend an aerobics class.

Buster & Booster #51

Put on a children's exercise video and follow along.

Buster & Booster #52

Go to the gym or YMCA, and keep your body moving.

Fidget

Fidgeting is a longstanding stress-relieving skill that is making a serious comeback. In 1996, during my senior year in high school, the *Tickle Me Elmo* doll was the hottest toy around. Stores could not keep them on the shelves, and scalpers were reportedly asking as much as $5,000 for the furry red monster.[7]

I remember thinking the Elmo craze was hilarious. However, last year, our youngest daughter received one of these nostalgic toys from her grandmother. After watching it in action, I have to admit the *Tickle Me Elmo* doll is cool. The point of this story is that fads catch on for a reason.

As I write this book, fidget spinners are the newest craze. It seems like every child carries at least two or three in their pockets at all times. Much to the dismay of adults, their familiar *whizzzzzzzzz* is heard in homes, classrooms, restaurants, parks, and shopping malls. Children cannot seem to get enough of this simple gadget. Yet, their popularity has a purpose. Children, as it turns out, have a profusion of excess energy.

With the reduction of physical education in schools and limits placed on the types of activities kids are allowed to play during recess — including bans on classic games like dodgeball and tag in some schools — it makes perfect sense that fidget spinners have caught on with a vengeance. Fortunately, these whirling plastic devices are not the only way for kids to release pent-up energy. The next set of stress busters and mood boosters provides simple fidgets that kids can use just about anywhere.

Buster & Booster #53

Twiddle your thumbs by interlock the fingers of both hands and twirling your thumbs in a circle.

> If this is too easy, switch things up by going in reverse too. I sometimes tell kids that this is the original fidget spinner.

Buster & Booster #54

Squeeze your hands tightly together for a few seconds. Then relax and repeat.

The physical act of tensing and relaxing is an excellent stress-relieving fidget. In class, kids can do this in a non-distracting manner by placing their hands underneath their desk and keeping their eyes directed toward the front of the room.

Buster & Booster #55

Use a fidget cube or stress ball.

Buster & Booster #56

Chew a stick of gum.

Buster & Booster #57

Bounce your leg.

Connect with Your Emotions

Clarifying one's feelings and experiencing them to the fullest is often the fastest route to the other side. Yet accomplishing this can be tricky, as feelings are fickle and incredibly confusing. In the animated movie *Home*, Oh, a purple alien voiced by Jim Parsons, attempts to understand human emotions. Oh asks his human companion, "So, you are sad-mad?" This fictional alien understands something that many people do not. Human beings are capable of experiencing two or more emotions simultaneously.

This can be especially confusing for kids. Taking simple steps to identify the emotion or emotions involved brings clarity to the situation and serves as a starting point for generating solutions. This section also offers strategies for sitting with the pain, because sometimes the fastest way through a dark place is straight through.

In regard to negative emotions, one of my favorite college professors often said, "It's just pain; it won't kill you."[8] Experiencing heartache, rage, confusion, and despair is difficult. Fortunately, the human body is not designed to endure the brunt of these emotions for long. Sit with the pain, and it will eventually pass. It is important to note that not every child can handle this. Yet, under the right conditions, it may be exactly what is needed.

I once heard a pastor preach an entire sermon on Luke 2:1a. This simple passage states, "It came to pass."[5] The preacher focused on how difficulties come and go. This pastor has a good point; intense feelings do indeed "come to pass," which makes waiting things out a viable stress-relieving option.

The next set of ideas helps children to identify their emotions and sit with the pain. This way they can move on to a bright future on the other side—a future so bright that they may need to wear shades!

Buster & Booster #58

Journal, and write your frustrations out.

Buster & Booster #59

Name the feelings you are experiencing, and list possible reasons you feel this way.

The simple act of verbalizing an emotion (or emotions) can bring clarity to the situation.

Buster & Booster #60

Cry it out.

Buster & Booster #61

Write a letter to the person you are upset with explaining why you are sad, angry, or frustrated, but don't send it.

The point of this exercise is for children to gain a better understanding of how they feel in the moment. Once written, the letter can be read to a parent or to another trusted adult.

Buster & Booster #62

Get creative by making a collage or sculpture of what you picture your anger, sadness, or frustration looks like.

Buster & Booster #63

Watch a sad movie, and sit with the feeling.

Be sure to pick a happy activity to transition to after the movie is over. This coping skill works because it allows kids to experience an emotion for a set period and then moves them forward.

Connect with Others

Kids need community. Cookies are better with milk, fish cannot survive without water, and children require close connections to others. Psychologist Harry Harlow drove this point home in the 1950s with his infamous experiment with rhesus monkeys. In a University of Wisconsin laboratory, Dr. Harlow separated infant monkeys from their families. He then offered the tiny creatures a choice between two machine mothers instead.

Both surrogates were formed from wire mesh. The first provided food, while the second was wrapped in soft terrycloth to provide comfort. Surprisingly, the animals spent most of their time clinging to the terrycloth mother. By choosing nurture over the security of keeping food nearby, these mammals debunked the myth that relationships are a luxury.

In a second experiment, Harry divided the monkeys into two groups. The first had access to the terrycloth mother, while the second group was left on its own. Next, loud noises were introduced to examine how these animals would manage stress. The first group responded by clinging tightly to the terrycloth mother. The second group, lacking the presence of nurturing support, rocked back and forth, screeched loudly, clutched themselves tightly, and cowered in fear. Without a support system nearby, their stress skyrocketed.

Harry filmed his experiments, and they are heart-wrenching to watch. Nevertheless, these procedures are worth remembering because they demonstrate the profound need for warm, caring connections. Parents, teachers, pastors, friends, coaches, and mentors all play a vital role in helping kids to bust stress and boost their moods. The next strategies provide ideas for helping kids make the most of their support network and alleviate stress by closely connecting with others.

Buster & Booster #64

Tell a safe friend how you feel.

The key word is "safe." Every feeling should not be shared with everyone. Instead, adults can help kids identify a group of compassionate friends and supportive adults with whom they can closely connect.

Buster & Booster #65

Phone a friend.

This lifeline from the popular game show *Who Wants to Be a Millionaire* works just as well in everyday life.

Buster & Booster #66

Ask for a hug.

Buster & Booster #67

Hug a stuffed animal or a pillow.

Dr. Harlow's experiment with rhesus monkeys demonstrates that when a caring human being is not around, a soft, cuddly surrogate will do.

Buster & Booster #68

Talk to your parents or grandparents.

Buster & Booster #69

Sit quietly with a friend.

Buster & Booster #70

Send out a social media SOS.

> This strategy should be used with caution. For older kids who are active on social media, posting a broad message requesting support is quite the rage. Although less than ideal, when monitored by a wise adult, this can help kids connect.

Buster & Booster #71

Schedule a time to talk to the most optimistic person you know.

Buster & Booster #72

Browse through a photo album filled with happy memories.

Some kids have difficulty recalling the good times and the positive people in their lives. When this is the case, creating a photo album can help them internalize their friendships and happy times.

Buster & Booster #73

Spend time with a pet.

Buster & Booster #74

Talk to a therapist, mentor, Sunday school teacher, or life coach.

Because kids may need to hear the same wisdom from multiple adults before taking it to heart, enlisting the support of others often helps.

Buster & Booster #75

Donate a toy to charity or to a child in need.

Supporting others is an excellent way to boost one's mood and often leads to developing positive relationships in the process.

Distract Yourself

Something that feels awful in the moment typically feels better a short time later. In my twenty-plus years of working with children, teens, and families, I have repeatedly found this to be true. After performing poorly on a test, thoughts of dropping out of school feel good. After arguing with a friend, ending the relationships feels like the right thing to do. And after cheating on a diet, bingeing for the remainder of the day feels best. *After all,* we say to ourselves, *since the diet is blown, I might as well enjoy the rest of the day.*

If any of these self-sabotaging behaviors sounds familiar, know that you are not alone. Although these illogical choices feel right, notice that *feels* is the key word. Because emotions change quickly, finding a distraction can prevent kids from making a rash decision that feels good in the moment but makes things worse in the future.

After an amygdala hijacking, it takes approximately twenty minutes for the frontal cortex to regain control. Even if a child appears calm, he or she may still not be in an optimal problem-solving state of mind. Fortunately, most difficulties don't need to be resolved immediately.

Wise adults might suggest, "You don't need to decide today. You can always give up, end the friendship, or make that bad choice tomorrow. For now, let's find something else to do." This next set of stress busters and mood boosters provides suggestions for helping kids step away from problems. Fortunately, disengaging—even for just a few moments—can make the world feel like a warmer place.

Buster & Booster #76

Engross yourself in a maze, crossword puzzle, or dot-to-dot.

Buster & Booster #77

Knit or weave.

Buster & Booster #78

Pause and count to 10.

Buster & Booster #79

Count backward from 100.

Buster & Booster #80

Do a jigsaw puzzle.

Buster & Booster #81

Garden.

Buster & Booster #82

Paint.

Buster & Booster #83

Bounce a balloon 100 times without letting it touch the floor.

If this is too easy, try it again using only your feet and knees to keep the balloon in the air.

Buster & Booster #84

Pop Bubble Wrap.

This is a favorite for many kids.

Buster & Booster #85

Sit by a lake, stream, or ocean.

Buster & Booster #86

Read a book or comic book.

Buster & Booster #87

Listen to an audiobook.

Engage the Senses

Some children respond especially well to sensory experiences. Just as each snowflake is unique, no two children are exactly alike. This is why psychology is an ongoing process of trial and error.

Back in graduate school, I took a psychopharmacology class. I was surprised to learn that even when it comes to something as delicate as prescribing medication, psychiatry is still a combination of science and art. Psychiatrists understand which medications typically work best for each set of symptoms. Nevertheless, there are never any guarantees. Once a medication appears to be working, the dosage is refined. On the other hand, if the results are poor, then a new prescription is tried.

Similarly, therapists are well versed in helping their clients discover the therapeutic tools that work best for them. Parents, teachers, and supportive adults who want to help kids manage stress and increase their mood must undergo a similar process of trial and error. Some children respond especially well to sensory experiences, which is why this next set of ideas hones in on sight, sound, smell, taste, and textures. The best way to know if these strategies will work for your child is to try them.

Buster & Booster #88

Rock in a rocking chair.

Buster & Booster #89

Play with modeling clay.

Buster & Booster #90

Smell a lemon or, better yet, make lemonade.

> The physical act of squeezing the lemons, combined with the vibrant smells, sweet taste of the sugar, and sour taste of the lemons all add to the sensory experience.

Buster & Booster #91

Squeeze putty or let slime drip through your fingers.

Buster & Booster #92

Crinkle tissue paper.

Buster & Booster #93

Shake a glitter jar and watch the contents settle.

> Glitter jars are a hot parenting trend. To make your own, add glitter, glitter glue, food coloring, and water to a clear plastic water bottle. Be sure to fasten the cap on tightly. The more glitter glue added, the longer it will take the concoction to settle. Watching the swirling glitter is a soothing sensory experience. Some parents have their child shake the bottle and take a break until the glitter is resettled, which typically takes between one to three minutes.

Buster & Booster #94

Finger paint.

Buster & Booster #95

Wear cozy pajamas or socks.

Buster & Booster #96

Wrap yourself in a warm blanket.

Buster & Booster #97

Make cloud-dough.

> Do this by combining 8 cups of flour with 1 cup of baby oil. Have kids mix the concoction with their hands. Cloud-dough smells great and is fun to play with too!

Change Your Scenery

A change of scenery is an excellent way to put problems back into their proper perspective. Shortly after graduating from college, I took up skydiving. Because of the high altitude of the jumps, the experience was more like floating than falling. The earth did not rush at me as expected. Instead, there was plenty of time to enjoy the view. As I gazed at the ocean, lakes, skyline, and stunning view below, problems melted away. The tiny bubble I lived in popped as I came face-to-face with the vastness, beauty, and awesomeness of our world!

Much to my dismay, I came to discover that purchasing my own parachute would cost more than paying off my car. This ended my stint of jumping out of airplanes. Of course, I am not suggesting that children go skydiving. There are plenty of safer and more cost-effective ways to assist kids in expanding their worldview. I share this story because most people can relate to getting caught up in a problem and then having an experience that jolts things back into perspective.

The human brain is adept at convincing kids that their challenges are massive. Changing their physical view can help them realize the universe is far bigger than the issues at hand. This next section provides ideas for encouraging kids to bust stress and boost their mood by altering their physical perspective.

Buster & Booster #98

Do a downward dog pose.

Buster & Booster #99

Do cartwheels or a handstand.

Buster & Booster #100

Hang upside down from monkey bars, or lay upside down on the couch.

Buster & Booster #101

Go for a bike or scooter ride.

Buster & Booster #102

Climb a tree.

Buster & Booster #103

Open the blinds.

Buster & Booster #104

Open all the windows in your home.

It is astounding what a little fresh air can do.

Buster & Booster #105

Spend time outside.

Buster & Booster #106

Volunteer at a soup kitchen or homeless shelter.

Supporting others in need is a superb way of helping kids keep their problems in proper perspective.

Buster & Booster #107

Go outside, lie on a blanket, and look up at the clouds.

Buster & Booster #108

Go for a walk at night, and gaze at the stars.

Try to identify constellations and search for shooting stars. To make this activity even more meaningful, spend a few moments researching the size of the universe in an encyclopedia or on the internet first. This can help kids grasp the magnitude of what they observe during their stargazing adventure.

Change Your Mental View

"There is nothing either good or bad, but thinking makes it so." This well-known quote from Shakespeare's *Hamlet* speaks to the power of changing one's mental outlook. As I stated earlier, Albert Ellis, the founder of Rational Emotive Behavior Therapy, used the terms *awfulizing* and *catastrophizing* to describe how focusing on a problem magnifies it. Michel de Montaigne said, "My life has been filled with terrible misfortune, most of which never happened." Sadly, many kids can say the same.

The good news is that changing one's mental perspective can pull kids out of this rut. This next set of stress busters and mood boosters focuses on thought-changing strategies that work especially well for children. Because each one requires some additional explanation, this section is longer than the previous ones. Yet these are some of my favorite tools, and learning them is worth the additional effort.

Buster & Booster #109

Squash ANTs.

ANTs is an acronym for automatic negative thoughts. Ants are annoying creatures that march into our homes, and ANTs are intrusive thoughts that invade our kids' minds. The solution is to recognize these buggers before they make mountains out of molehills. Then squash them by replacing the negative thoughts with more rational, positive ones.

Buster & Booster #110

Reframe the problem.

Have you noticed how a picture that does not look quite right suddenly fits nicely after the frame is changed? Mental reframing is similar. A problem viewed as "awful" can be reframed as an "adventure," "an opportunity for growth," or "a normal part of growing up." The next set of stress busters and mood boosters contains some of my favorite reframes. Of course, you can always create your own too.

Buster & Booster #111

Tell yourself: *This is an adventure.*

> Instead of viewing struggles as a catastrophe, decide they are an adventure. After all, it is likely you will make new friends, develop valuable skills, and make fascinating discoveries along the way.

Buster & Booster #112

Tell yourself: *This is a learning experience and an opportunity for growth.*

> Failing a test, losing a friendship, or coming in last place does not have to lead to despair. Children can use the experience as an opportunity for growth, choosing to fail forward instead. After all, most childhood blunders are fairly easy to bounce back from, making this the ideal time for mistakes.

Buster & Booster #113

Tell yourself: *I am a survivor.*

> Kids can decide not to be a victim and choose to view themselves as a survivor instead. This is an excellent reframe for children who have experienced trauma. The bright side is that

children are resilient. I like this reframe because it takes the spotlight off tragedy and places it on one's ability to bounce back stronger and wiser than ever before.

Buster & Booster #114

Tell yourself: *This is a good story that will help a lot of people one day.*

I like this reframe because it hones in on how a challenging story can be used to inspire others.

Buster & Booster #115

Tell yourself: *It is an experiment.* Then, get curious about the results.

I love the classic picture of the mad scientist holding a beaker in each hand. There is usually a mischievous smile on his face because this scientist knows he is about to make an important discovery. He may find a formula that turns lead into gold, or the concoction could explode. Either way, once the beakers are mixed, this scientist will be a little bit wiser. Instead of stressing, help children adopt the mad scientist attitude.

View new endeavors as an experiment. Then, grow from the results.

Buster & Booster #116

Identify ways that life is unfair to your advantage.

"Life is not fair." This is a concept that adults frequently attempt to pass on to kids. The implication is "You better learn to deal with difficulties because life is unfairly against you." However, life can also be unfair in a child's favor. For example, living in the United States (one of the wealthiest and freest nations on earth) and having good health and a loving family are all undeserved blessings. Adults can help children boost their mood by encouraging them to identify ways that life is unfair to their advantage.

Buster & Booster #117

Use softer language when describing negative events.

A primary concept of Neural Linguistic Programming, or NLP for short, is that feelings are connected to language. When kids describe their circumstances as "horrible" or "terrible," their mood adjusts to fit this intensity. On the other hand, when softer language is employed, by using words like "disappointing" or "mildly frustrating," the emotional impact is lessened. NLP does not suggest that kids should pretend the world is all rainbows and unicorns. Instead, it promotes reducing the emotional impact of negative events by softening one's language.

Buster & Booster #118

Get energized by using power words to describe positive life events.

On a similar note, NLP teaches that words also energize. Tell a child, "You did well," and he or she will smile. Proclaim, "You studied hard for that test and did awesome!" and that child's face will light up. Words tell our brain how to feel. Using vibrant, uplifting language will not only cause you to feel empowered but soon the kids around you will follow suit.

Buster & Booster #119

Embrace your imperfections, rough edges, and mistakes by being thankful for them.

Imperfect people connect best with other imperfect people. On the one hand, nonstick pans are excellent cooking utensils, because their smooth coating allows burned foods to slide right off. On the other hand, a smooth coating is less desirable for human beings. Kids need to know that rough edges, failures, and humanness are what allow relationships to stick. Therefore, instead of hiding imperfections, embrace them. Admittedly, this is a big concept for children to grasp. Yet it is never too early to begin teaching this invaluable mood-boosting lesson.

Practice Good Self-Talk

People tell themselves how to act and what to feel. If you don't believe me, try this experiment. The next time you feel down, attempt to identify the specific thoughts running through your mind. Chances are they are negative and self-defeating. These thoughts may include statements like:

- *This is too hard.*

- *I will never figure it out.*

- *Someone else would be better at this than I would.*

Kids use this type of negative self-talk all the time. Adults can help kids bust stress and boost their mood by teaching them simple self-talk statements to use throughout the day. One way to accomplish this is by repeating these phrases aloud at opportune times.

I had a professor do this in college. Then one day, when it felt like I would never reach the graduation finish line, one of his famous phrases popped into my head. I was surprised to find that my self-talk contained this professor's exact tone and inflections. It was as if he was standing right next to me.

This wise psychology professor had gotten inside my head, and it was just what I needed to continue pressing forward. In this section, you will find some of my favorite self-talk statements for kids. Feel free to use the ones I provide or create your own.

Buster & Booster #120

Tell yourself, *Go slow, be patient, and take your time.*

> Kids increase their troubles by reacting too quickly. Most problems do not need to be resolved right now, and trying only generates additional chaos. When emotions run high, one of the best things children can do is to remind themselves to go slow, be patient, and take their time. In the classic story of "The Tortoise and the Hare," the tortoise wins every time. Slow and steady is a recipe for winning in countless areas of life.

Buster & Booster #121

Tell yourself, *Oops, maybe next time.*

This self-talk statement reminds kids to view errors as fixable. In fact, childhood is one of the best times to make mistakes because kids nearly always have another opportunity to get things right.

Buster & Booster #122

Remind yourself, *Trust the process*.

Doing the work leads to achieving the goal. This self-talk statement reminds kids to complete what they are asked to do without protest, trusting that the process will lead them to what they desire. "Trust the process" is the phrase that inspired me to keep pressing forward when I was discouraged, so I know the power of this simple statement.

Practice Self-Care

Self-care energizes us so we can encourage others. My first car was a 1987 Suzuki Swift. Although this two-door, four-seat hatchback was a tight fit for my six-foot frame, I did not mind. For me, this car equaled freedom. Then one day, the car wouldn't start. Unsure of what to do next, I walked into the house to think. When I returned, the engine fired right up. *Did I simply imagine my car not starting?* I wondered to myself.

A week later, the problem resurfaced. After turning the key in the ignition, the engine remained silent. As a naive college student, I decided the best course of action was to ignore the issue for the second time. When I returned a short time later, the engine once again effortlessly ignited.

This ridiculous routine went on for some months. Since I was ultimately able to get to where I wanted to go, I figured I could live with the delays. My only real concern was that each week the condition grew worse.

Eventually, I decided to take my car to a mechanic. It turns out the vehicle had a bad starter. The mechanic explained that the problem would escalate until the part was replaced. Understanding this finally caused me to take action. With a fresh starter, the engine ignited with every turn of the key.

Some kids treat their physical bodies similar to the way I treated my first car. They stay up late, eat far too much junk food, and don't practice good personal hygiene. This leads to lethargy and difficulties appearing bigger than they are. In other words, these kids have starter problems and, as I did, are choosing to ignore them. Unfortunately, this lack of appropriate self-care leads to decreased energy, enthusiasm, and get-up-and-go.

Contrary to popular belief, self-care is not selfish. Instead, it energizes kids so they can encourage others. I love walking into our home at the end of the day. No matter how challenging my day has been, hearing my four girls squeal with delight, "Daddy is home," always renews my joy. Yet, energizing others is only possible when kids take care of themselves first.

As in previous sections, many of these stress-busting and mood-boosting strategies are common sense. Nevertheless, they are included in this book because children often fail to practice the invaluable skills they already know. This next section provides self-care strategies to help kids reduce stress and feel better about themselves so they can refresh others.

Buster & Booster #123

Eat a healthy snack—especially if you are hangry.

"Hangry," or hungry-angry, is a new expression that acknowledges that one's appetite is connected to his or her mood. Not all kids recognize their body's signals. Adults can help kids boost their mood by assisting them in identifying and meeting their physical needs.

Buster & Booster #124

Go to bed early and sleep on it.

When it comes to resolving problems, very little good happens after 8 p.m. I share this wisdom with parents, and Jenny and I readily apply it in our own home. Yet there is a delicate balance to this. On the one hand, bedtime is when children are most ready to talk, making evenings an excellent time to learn about their day. On the other hand, nighttime is also when problem-solving is the most difficult. If you catch your child growing increasingly emotional, don't be afraid to say, "Honey, why don't you get some sleep. We can talk more in the morning." It is truly astounding how a good night's rest can improve a child's entire outlook on life.

Buster & Booster #125

Get a haircut, trim your nails, or get a pedicure.

Buster & Booster #126

Start each day by making your bed.

In his bestselling book, *Make Your Bed: Little Things That Can Change Your Life. . . And Maybe Even the World*,[9] William McRaven suggests that beginning each day by completing a small task with excellence—such as making one's bed—sets a tone of excellence for the remainder of the day. This simple idea is pure genius and worth passing on to kids.

Buster & Booster #127

Say no.

This is also known as setting good boundaries. Because kids have more options than ever before, they must become adept at saying no. Otherwise, all the available selections can overwhelm them. In our home, Jenny and I teach our kids to say no to some good things, to make time to say yes to great opportunities that come their way.

Choose Wisely

Happy kids focus on how they can improve their situation, as opposed to trying to get what they want by beguiling others. William Glasser, the founder of Choice Theory, refers to attempts to control, bribe, and manipulate others as *external control psychology*. According to Glasser, external control psychology does not work because it always harms the relationship, and relationship problems are at the root of nearly all human miseries.

Glasser's solution is simple. Instead of attempting to change others, focus on the positive choices you can make instead. My third-grade teacher proclaimed, "When you point the finger at someone else, you have three fingers pointing back at you." This is Glasser's wisdom stated at a child's level. Children are not helpless, and most kids have more options than they realize. This next set of strategies inspires children to bust stress and boost their mood by taking their eyes off others and focusing on the choices they can make.

Buster & Booster #128

Decide on the best course of action by creating a pros-and-cons list.

This simple but powerful tool can help children make wise choices when deciding is difficult. Start by folding a sheet of notebook paper in half. Then write the pros of the decision on one side and the cons on the other. Looking at a decision from this perspective can provide clarity on what to do next.

Buster & Booster #129

Take one small step toward resolving the problem.

The purpose of this strategy is to build momentum. Without momentum, making progress feels like wading through a swimming pool full of cold, sticky syrup—advancement is slow and gaining headway requires a great deal of effort. However, once momentum is in our kid's favor, progress feels like a downhill sled ride. Adults can help kids build momentum by assisting them in breaking down their goals into small, actionable steps. Then encourage them to reach their goal one small step at a time.

Buster & Booster #130

Forgive.

It is said that unforgiveness is like drinking poison and hoping the other person feels sick. In other words, when kids hold on to past hurts, they injure themselves the most. Adults can help kids boost their happiness by teaching them to let go, forgive, and move on.

Mood-Booster Stacking

After practicing the basic ideas in this book, kids can level up their stress-busting and mood-boosting abilities by stacking their favorite strategies together. While reading this book, perhaps you have found yourself thinking, *I have tried these strategies before, and they don't work*. Unfortunately, raising kids — even extraordinarily good kids — requires hard labor and intentional effort.

The good news is that there is always something new to try, which is one of the reasons for including so many ideas in this book. However, if you still find yourself discouraged, then it may be time for the next steps.

First, understand that change is difficult. More often than not, bad habits form over a period of months or years, which mean they will take significant time to break. Growth most often occurs in small spurts, with periods of regression along the way. If this is true in your family, then congratulations, you are normal. A patient persistence, coupled with an enthusiastic belief that change is possible, is a powerful ally on this journey.

So keep practicing these skills with your kids, and continue pressing forward. Second, although most of the stress busters and mood boosters in this book are simple, know that helping your kids learn them is only the beginning. The next step is to practice stacking these skills together. A child might do this by taking a deep breath, walking away from a negative situation, changing his or her self-talk using one of the phrases provided, and then going for a brisk walk to burn off any excess frustration. This is an example of using four strategies in tandem, and it produces a dynamic mood-boosting effect!

Buster & Booster #131

Stack your favorite strategies together to build massive stress-busting, mood-boosting momentum.

Helping Kids
Fully Recharge

Gracefully navigating stressful situations is easiest when kids are already in a positive mood. Have you ever woken up from a full night's rest feeling rejuvenated and indomitable—as if you could conquer any difficulty that comes your way? If so, then you probably already understand the value of the advice in this chapter.

Although coping skills are an excellent way for kids to bust stress and boost their mood in the moment, children also require longer breaks to recharge fully. Not long ago, I stepped out of the hustle and bustle of my standard routine, and this break reminded me of the significance of unmitigated downtime.

After spending nearly twenty hours tied to a tree in an isolated patch of snow-covered forest, I feel great. My thoughts are clear. My mind is bursting with fresh ideas. Everything around me seems vivid and alive. *I can't wait to do this again next year,* I enthusiastically think to myself.

My father-in-law calls this experience hunting, and technically, I wasn't tied to a tree but clipped into a deer stand fifteen feet above the woodland floor. Nevertheless, for the majority of that weekend, a lone tree was my abode. When I returned home, my wife, Jenny, who was raised in Minnesota and is used to the deer-hunting obsession, declared, "I don't get it. What draws guys to hunting?"

Of course, there was a time when hunting was done out of pure necessity. Providing for one's family entailed killing something and dragging it home. However, today, with grocery stores in every city and fast-food restaurants on most corners, this need no longer exists.

For me, one major draw is tranquility. Uninterrupted stillness is a rare commodity. In fact, it is so rare that the first few hours alone with my thoughts were difficult. Then the magic happened. As I sat in the incessant stillness, I could almost feel my body recharging. In a world of frenzied movement, hunting became my excuse to be still.

Thinking Holidays

A therapist I know tells the story of a family friend who went through an especially challenging time in his life. The friend reported that he stopped taking his prescribed medication because the drugs made it difficult to think. After a particularly stressful day, this man reached his breaking point and began acting in ways that were drastically out of character. Fortunately, my therapist friend was nearby and suggested this man permit himself to take a thinking holiday. After this conversation, the man checked himself into a hospital and resumed his prescribed medication.

Although this story is an extreme example, I share it because all of us need an occasional thinking holiday. This is true for both adults and kids. Whether the break comes in the form of a day off from school, an extended vacation, or a weekend hunting excursion, finding longer ways to regenerate is crucial.

Discovering Your Child's Tree

What is your child's tree? How does he or she step out of the hustle and bustle of life to recharge? These are important questions to ask because coping skills are less potent if your child is continually running near empty. It may be helpful to picture coping skills as a daily multivitamin that alleviates but does not cure. If it has been an especially stressful year, taking additional time to recuperate before implementing the ideas in this book may be warranted.

Busting Stress in a Changing World

In my previous book, *131 Boredom Busters and Creativity Builders for Kids*, I share our family's journey from overly entertained and hyper-scheduled to finding a more balanced approach to life. In 2014, some articles were published referring to the micro-generation born between 1977 and 1983 as Xennials. Since this is my generation, the term caught my eye, and the articles reminded me how quickly the world changes. Xennials are "the last kids to make it all the way to grown up without pervasive technology."[10]

For today's children, smartphones, laptops, and wireless internet are the norm. Of course, as society progresses, strategies for helping kids bust stress and boost their mood must advance too. The days when parents had to seek out activities for their children are long gone. Today, it is a matter of deciding which sports, hobbies, and interests our children will join, out of a multitude of options available. While this progress is not bad, adults need to be aware that kids are growing up in a far different world than they remember.

A World without Walls

In middle school, I heard a speaker relay the following story:

> Growing up is like traversing down a narrow hallway. When my generation were kids, the hallway doors were closed, and most were locked. My friends and I would occasionally hear other children talk about sex, alcohol, drugs, and engaging in other subversive activities. However, most of

these things were not easily accessible. For your generation, it is as if the doors of this hallway are unlocked and cracked open. Dangers and pitfalls are more readily available to you than they were for me.

If this was true for my generation, then our kids have the doors, and perhaps even the walls, of this hallway removed entirely. Open internet access and broader access to information in general put a wealth of knowledge at our kids' fingertips. As with most changes, these advances have both their pros and cons. The aim is not to build fear but to create awareness. Because the world is continually changing, adults need to adapt in the ways they support kids in managing stress.

Practice Makes Perfect

Stress-busting, mood-boosting skills are more likely to be caught than taught. If you begin by regulating your own emotions, the kids around you will begin to follow your example. Although this book is written specifically for parents and educators who desire to assist children in self-regulating, these ideas work for adults too. In fact, when I present these strategies to families, parents often state, "I think all of us will benefit from this."

In This Together

You and I are on this journey of equipping our children, with a host of other parents, teachers, and mentors. So be encouraged, knowing that you are not alone. Helping children learn to exert effortful control over their emotions is indeed an ongoing process. As my former college professor, Dr. Lord, would say, "Trust the process." Start by teaching these skills to your children. Then model and practice them daily. Finally, reinforce progress with hearty praise every time you catch a child putting one of these skills into action.

As we have seen, healthy relationships, career success, and overall happiness are tied to a child's ability to manage his or her emotions. In short, self-regulating kids possess greater odds of excelling virtually everywhere. So keep pressing forward, because the rewards are worth the effort. I continue to wish you and the kids in your care much success in this ongoing stress-busting and mood-boosting journey!

End Notes

1. James Clear, "40 Years of Stanford Research Found That People With This One Quality Are More Likely to Succeed," James Clear, accessed January 1, 2018 https://jamesclear.com/delayed-gratification.
2. "The Marshmallow Test," YouTube, last modified September 24, 2009, https://www.youtube.com/watch?v=QX_oy9614HQ.
3. Robert L. Leahy, *The Worry Cure: Seven Steps to Stop Worry from Stopping You* (New York: Harmony, 2005).
4. David G. Myers, *Psychology*, 9th ed. (New York: Worth, 2010).
5. Scripture quoted by permission. All scripture quotations, unless otherwise indicated, are taken from the NET Bible® copyright ©1996-2017 by Biblical Studies Press, L.L.C. All rights reserved.
6. Robert Emmons and Michael McCullough, "Highlights from the Research Project on Gratitude and Thankfulness, accessed January 1, 2018, http://citeseerx.ist.psu.edu/viewdoc/download?doi=10.1.1.520.4351&rep=rep1&type=pdf.
7. Jonathan Silverstine, "Tickle Me Elmos Selling for $5,000," ABC News, published October 19, 2006, http://abcnews.go.com/Technology/story?id=2583572&page=1%0c
8. Quote attributed to Dr. Barry Lord, quoted from this author's memory.

9. William McRaven, *Make Your Bed: Little Things That Can Change Your Life... And Maybe Even the World* (New York: Grand Central, 2017).

10. Trisha Leigh Zeigenhorn, "There's Now a Name for the Micro Generation Born Between 1977-1983" *Did You Know?*, last modified June 27, 2017, http://didyouknowfacts.com/theres-now-a-name-for-the-micro-generation-born-between-1977-1983/

Thumbs Up or Thumbs Down

Thank you for purchasing this book!

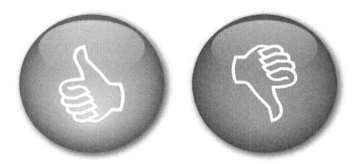

I would love to hear from you. Your feedback not only helps me grow as a writer, but it also helps me get books into the hands of those who need them most. Online reviews are one of the biggest ways that independent authors — like me — connect with new readers.

If you loved the book, could you please share your experience? Leaving feedback is as easy as answering any of these questions:

- What did you like about the book?

- What is your most important takeaway or insight?

- What have you done differently — or what will you do differently because of what you have read?

- To whom would you recommend this book?

Of course, I am looking for honest reviews. So if you have a minute to share your experience, good or bad, please consider leaving a review!

I look forward to hearing from you!

Sincerely,

COFFEE SHOP CONVERSATIONS

About the Author

Jed is passionate about helping people live happier, healthier, more connected lives by having better conversations. He is a husband, a father of four girls, a psychology professor, therapist, and writer.

Jed graduated from Southern California Seminary with a Master of Divinity and returned to complete a second master's degree in psychology. In his free time, Jed enjoys walking on the beach, reading, and spending time with his incredible family.

Continue the Conversation

If you enjoyed this book, I would love it if you would leave a review. Your feedback is an awesome encouragement to me, and it helps books like this one get noticed. It only takes a minute, and every review is greatly appreciated. Oh, and please feel free to stay in touch too!

Email: jed@coffeeshopconversations.com

Twitter: @jjurchenko

Facebook: Coffee Shop Conversations

Blog: www.CoffeeShopConversations.com

More Family Books

This book and other creative conversation starters are available at www.Amazon.com.

Transform your relationship from dull and bland to inspired, passionate, and connected as you grow your insights into your partner's inner world! Whether you are newly dating or nearing your golden anniversary, these questions are for you. This book will help you share your heart and better know your partner.

131 Creative Conversations for Couples

More Family Books

Engage your teenagers and connect like never before! This book is packed with creative conversation starters that will guide you on the journey.

These conversation starters for parents and teens are founded on Biblical principles and reinforce positive values. Some conversation starters are faith-based. Others are fun and funny. All of them promote connection and growth.

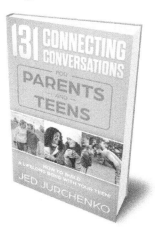

131 Connecting Conversation for Parents and Teens

Made in the USA
Coppell, TX
01 June 2021

56717276R00138